the
ROAD TO SUCCESS
is
PAVED WITH HARDSHIPS

DEBRAKAY M. BROWN

THE ROAD TO SUCCESS IS PAVED WITH HARDSHIPS. Copyright © 2025. Debrakay M. Brown. All Rights Reserved.

Printed in the United States of America.

No portion of this book may be reproduced, stored in a retrieval system, or transmitted in any form or by any means, except for brief quotations in printed reviews, without the prior written permission of DayeLight Publishers or Debrakay M. Brown.

ISBN: 978-1-958443-98-9 (paperback)

Scripture quotations marked "KJV" are taken from the Holy Bible, King James Version (Public Domain).

Scripture quotations marked (NIV) are taken from the Holy Bible, New International Version®, NIV®. Copyright © 1973, 1978, 1984 by Biblica, Inc.™ Used by permission of Zondervan. All rights reserved worldwide.

Scripture quotations marked (NLT) are taken from the Holy Bible, New Living Translation, copyright © 1996, 2004, 2007 by Tyndale House Foundation. Used by permission of Tyndale House Publishers, Inc., Carol Stream, Illinois 60188. All rights reserved.

Scripture quotations marked "NKJV" are taken from the New King James Version. Copyright © 1982 by Thomas Nelson, Inc. Used by permission. All rights reserved. Bible text from the New King James Version® is not to be reproduced in copies or otherwise by any means except as permitted in writing by Thomas Nelson, Inc., Attn: Bible Rights and Permissions, P.O. Box 141000, Nashville, TN 37214-1000.

Scripture quotations marked "ESV" are from the ESV Bible® (The Holy Bible, English Standard Version®), copyright © 2001 by Crossway Bibles, a publishing ministry of Good News Publishers. Used by permission. All rights reserved.

Scripture quotations taken from the Amplified® Bible (AMP). Copyright © 2015 by The Lockman Foundation. Used by permission. www.Lockman.org.

Acknowledgments

I want to express my deepest gratitude to those who encouraged and assisted me throughout this journey. It was a huge undertaking, but with all the help and support I received, everything worked out well. I am now officially an author.

My heartfelt thanks to my immediate family for their encouragement, support, and love. Your belief in me certainly motivated me on this journey.

Special thanks to my husband, Rev. Verniel Brown, for everything you have done to help me realize my dreams. You patiently assisted in research, provided and sanctioned Bible references and supporting scriptures, and verified Bible facts and verses I utilized. Your help was priceless. You also catered to my meals, ensuring I ate even when I did not remember eating. I will never forget you taking off my glasses when I fell asleep with my pen and book in my hand. I was amused when you shared pictures of me fast asleep in awkward positions. Your contribution to this book has enhanced it in many ways.

Thanks to my daughter, Joseian Brown Edwards (RN, BSN), for assisting me in formatting and arranging the book in the correct sequence so I could submit it for official editing and proofreading.

Thanks for putting up with my frequent request of calling you and saying, "One minute, Jo." Those one minutes turned out to be several minutes. Your insight as a NICU nurse has helped me understand the dedication and strength required for the work you do, and the facts you gave me helped me to compare the life of a NICU nurse to The Road to Success Paved with Hardships.

To my son, Sgt. Verniel D. Brown, who is presently serving the United States of America, thanks a million for the significant help you gave me in supplying me with vital facts that I was able to use as I likened the life of a soldier to a path lined with obstacles on this road to success.

I want to say thanks to my three grandchildren, Jomarah (JJ), Jamaal (Mally) and Nia (Nini), for their contribution to my book.

Thanks to JJ, an enthusiastic sunset lover who spends each evening capturing the breathtaking beauty of the sky as day turns to night. With her eye for color, she collects stunning photographs that highlight vibrant hills and serene moments of twilight. She shared one of these photographs with me, which became the beautiful sunset on the cover of my book. This input invites readers to experience the sunset through her lens and to realize that there is always beauty beyond the dark clouds.

My younger granddaughter, Nia (Nini), thank you for your incredible drawing of cactus plants that you encouraged me to include on the front cover of this book. Your exact drawing was not used, but your idea was used to include the cactus on the front cover of my book, adding a touch of warmth and inspiration that perfectly complements the themes within. Your suggestion shines through in every detail and beautifully illustrates the journey of overcoming rough roads to success. While the prickles on the cactus may represent challenges, the vibrant beauty of the cacti reminds us that there is always something wonderful to be found, even in tough circumstances. I am happy to have your creativity as a reminder of resilience and beauty.

My only grandson, Jamaal (Mally), is a young football player whose journey reflects a path to success paved with determination and resilience. His dedication to this sport, despite the challenges he faces, inspires me deeply. Every practice session and game he prepares for tells a story of hard work, perseverance, and the will to overcome obstacles. Watching him chase his dreams is a powerful reminder that success is often forged through struggles, and his spirit motivates me to capture that essence in my writing.

All three grandkids never failed to check in with me to find out how my writing was going. My grandson promised to be the first person to read my book when it is published.

Before I began authoring my book, I sought advice from my wonderful mentor, my close friend, Reverend Dr. Dalton Jenkins. He was helpful and kind with his knowledge and expertise as an author himself. He spent precious time counseling me on the best course to pursue to be a successful author; I salute you, sir.

I extend my deepest gratitude to the incredible community whose support played a crucial role in this book's success and everyone who participated in the questionnaires; your insight and time were invaluable.

Thank you to those who stayed connected and sent a motivational quote or a word of cheer through phone calls. Your encouragement and feedback kept me motivated every step of the way.

Special thanks to the sponsors whose generosity made this project possible. I am deeply grateful. It is as much your book as it is mine.

I would love to include the names of my contributors who inspired this work: Ms. N. Adams (Principal Director of Corporate Services

(J.W.I.), Jennifer Andrews (GA), Marlene Brown (GA), Mr. &Mrs. N. Williams (GA), Mrs. D. Harvey-Burrell (J.W.I.), Mr. & Mrs. E. Clarke (GA), Mrs. P. Currie (BX), Ms. Marcia Gayle (GA), Mr. & Mrs. D. Hall (Grand Cayman), Ms. T. Hart (BX), Ms. Y. Hibbert (GA), Mrs. D. Seymore (GA), Mrs. I. McLean (GA), Mr. & Mrs. G. Pusey (England), Mr. R. Smith (GA), Mrs. A. Depass-Thomas (GA), Ms. Janel Thorpe (GA), Ms. H. Bailey (GA), Mr. & Mrs. R. Hawthorne (GA), Mr. J. Smith (WA), Ms. A. Burrell (MA), and Ms. T. McKoy (FL).

To the team at DayeLight Publishers, with specific mention of the director and CEO, Ms. Crystal Daye, BSc. CEO, bestselling author, your dedication, commitment, and vision have shone brightly through this process. You and your team have been a guiding light throughout the publishing journey. From the first manuscript submission to the final print, you and your team have been both professional and inspiring. Your belief in the potential of this book has given me the confidence to bring it to life. Your meticulous diligence, creative insights, and consistent communication have made this process smooth and incredibly rewarding; I thank you.

To my illustrator, your illustrations brought my words to life in a way I could never have imagined; thank you. Your talent and vision are remarkable. I really could not have asked for a better collaboration. Thank you for your dedication and hard work.

I am forever grateful to the designer whose creativity brought my book and vision to reality; I am so excited to share the final product with all my readers.

To my photographer, Mrs. Latoya Hawthorne-Stiner, thank you for the incredible photograph you took for my book cover and "Meet the

Author" page. Your talent and vision brought it to life. I am grateful for your contribution.

Thanks to my readers and everyone who believed in this project. Your work means more than my frail words can express. The encouragement was invaluable. Your belief in me throughout this journey kept me going during the most challenging times.

May you all be especially blessed.

Table of Contents

Acknowledgments iii
Introduction 11
Discover the Author Behind the Words 13
Chapter 1: The Road to Success is Paved With Hardships 15
Chapter 2: Difficulties To be Encountered on the Road to Success. 21
Chapter 3: A Glance at This Road to Success 35
Chapter 4: A Mirror Synopsis Of My Journey 47
Chapter 5: A Faithful God 73
Chapter 6: Trials to Triumph 81
Chapter 7: The Triumph of Resilience 95
Chapter 8: Different Seasons on the Journey to Success 113
Chapter 9: Guiding Signs on the Road to Success 127
Chapter 10: The Life of a Soldier Compared to the Road to Success Paved With Hardships 153
Chapter 11: The Life of a Sailor Compared to the Road to Success Paved With Hardships 161
Chapter 12: The Life of a Jeweler Compared to the Road to Success Paved With Hardships 167
Chapter 13: The Life of a Baker Compares to the Road to Success Paved With Hardships 171
Chapter 14: Life in the Medical Field Compared With the Road to Success Paved With Hardships 173

Chapter 15: The Life of a Farmer Compared to The Road to Success is Paved With Hardships 175

Chapter 16: The Life of a Builder Compared With The Road to Success Paved With Hardships 177

Chapter 17: The Life of a Teacher Compared to the Road to Success Paved With Hardships 179

Chapter 18: The Life of a Musician Compared to the Road to Success Paved With Hardships 181

Chapter 19: The Life of a Neonatal Intensive Care (NICU) Nurse Compared to the Road to Success Paved With Hardships 183

Chapter 20: Requirements For A Successful Journey 185

Questionnaire Mrs. P 189

Questionnaire Lady L 193

Questionnaire Ms. N. 201

Questionnaire Mrs. D 207

Summary Of The Road To Success Is Paved With Hardships 213

Pray This Prayer Daily 219

Introduction

Success is frequently portrayed as a straightforward and seamless path, but it is significantly less complicated.

I welcome you to this book, **"The Road to Success is Paved With Hardships."**

I would like you to learn more about what success means and the challenges that stand in the way of our achievements and ultimate greatness.

This book explores narratives and tactics that demonstrate our adversity. Rather than just being a barrier, it is essential to the happiness of our achievement.

Using words of perspectives and experiences, we will explore our tenacity, resolve, and unwavering spirit, which may transform obstacles into opportunities.

Every segment of this book should provide useful guidance based on authentic biblical and real-world stories and experiences, enabling you to walk this path confidently.

I implore you to get on this journey that redefines success, embracing the trials and tribulations as components of a rewarding and meaningful pursuit.

Debrakay M. Brown

Through exploration, you will gain a deeper appreciation for the strength and growth that emerge from overcoming adversity.

I welcome you to the journey where the road to success is illuminated by the various hardships that forge our greatest achievements.

Discover the Author Behind the Words

With great pleasure, I present Debrakay Brown, a brilliant new literary voice. Although the path to achievement is filled with obstacles, she contributes a wealth of life experience to her debut book, "The Road to Success is Paved with Hardships."

Over the years, she has influenced innumerable youngsters and adults as a resolute teacher, now retired. She is married to Rev. Verniel T. Brown, is the mother of two amazing children, and is the grandmother of three astounding grandchildren. She majors in music and religious education. She enjoys singing, writing poems, plays, short stories, and listening to music.

Through her book, Debrakay hopes to inspire others to embrace their challenges and turn them into opportunities for success.

Kindly join her on this transformative journey and discover the power of perseverance and hope.

Chapter 1

The Road to Success is Paved With Hardships

I want to define each word in the above heading. According to the Oxford Dictionary, the word **'the'** refers to donating one or more individuals or things that have already been mentioned or are supposed to be common knowledge.

According to the Oxford Lexicon, the word **'road'** refers to a wide path that can be used by automobiles and humans.

The Oxford Dictionary states that the term **'to'** expresses mobility in the direction of a specific location.

The Oxford Dictionary defines **'success'** as accomplishing an aim or purpose.

The word **'is'** is in the third person singular or the present tense to be one and two.

'Paved,' according to the same Oxford dictionary, means to cover an area or ground with a hard, flat surface of pieces of stone or concrete or bricks.

The word **'with,'** according to the Oxford Dictionary, means being in the same place as someone or something else.

According to the Oxford Dictionary, **'hardship'** is a condition that is difficult to endure, such as pain, deprivation, oppression, or a life of struggle.

The road to success is typically described as an arduous path or trip. It is critical to remain constantly aware of the numerous problems that may arise along this route.

In a world that often glorifies the results of success—the accolades, wealth, and recognition—it is extremely easy to overlook the often-unseen journey that leads to those achievements. This book, "**The Road to Success is Paved With Hardships,**" invites you to explore the profound truth that struggles and adversities are not merely obstacles to be overcome but vital components of growth and resilience. This book chronicles the stories of individuals, including me, who faced significant challenges, illustrating how their hardships shaped their path and forged their character.

Through their experiences, we will uncover the lessons learned in the crucible of adversity, revealing that success is not a straight line but a winding road filled with trials that lead to greater understanding, strength, and fulfillment.

There are numerous obstacles on the road to success. We will look at some of the most common ones you may encounter. Some of these are fear of failure, lack of motivation, self-doubt, pitfalls, challenging circumstances, thinking negatively, losing focus, not accepting changes well, over-extending oneself, and lack of support, to name a few.

You will learn about others as you reach further in this book. Irrespective of the circumstances, giving up should be the farthest thing from our minds. To overcome these problems, specific goals must be established. There must be a plan of action. First, remaining focused is critical to excellent achievement and wonderful outcomes. The key to success on this journey is to believe in yourself and stay motivated, continuously reminding yourself of your aspirations daily. This is a great strategy. Mistakes and hiccups will inevitably occur along the way, but they should not stop you when things go wrong. Attempt to discover your mistakes right away; however, never dwell on your mistakes; rather, seize every opportunity to improve yourself.

The route to success is constantly being renovated, so pay attention and remain steadfast on your goals; this will result in a profitable outcome. Some road surfaces themselves will have more challenges than others, but all we need to do is stay grounded, keep a calm head, and focus on our goals, and we should achieve the outcome we desire.

The key to success on this road is to believe in yourself. Mistakes and setbacks will be on the path; however, these should not be a deterrent. Find out how you can learn from your mistakes; examine and decide what you could have done differently. Once you have learned from your mistakes, apply those lessons to achieve success in the days, weeks, and years to come.

When you achieve your victories, celebrate yourself, and do not look at small victories insignificantly; these should lead you to long-term goals. Remember that success is not just a destination; it is a long, jerky, rough journey filled with difficulties, and victory is in the end.

Determination is what is needed. This requires much effort and perseverance to reach maximum capacity. Create and develop a plan; make an investment in yourself, stay confident and motivated, and navigate your road to success. Success is a personal journey that no one can travel for you. You must do it all by yourself, creating and maintaining the right mindset and willingness to learn to overcome obstacles and achieve your self-tailored version of success.

Set goals that are realistic and are aligned with your strengths. Sometimes, your attempt at success may result in failure, but should this happen, there is no need to panic. Accept the reality, analyze your failure, find strategies, and use your skills to correct errors. Always avoid making rash decisions but gradually advance to corrective measures.

Exercise resilience and determination while you are navigating your way on what can be described as the rough and murky waters on this journey to success. Navigate your course gracefully and meticulously. You can never get rid of setbacks, but never allow unfavorable situations to break your self-confidence and self-esteem. They should make you stronger. At the same time, they should build your spiritual muscles and increase your level of endurance.

The importance of making the effort to press forward without giving up cannot be overstated. This resilience is vital in unlocking a secure and more confident you. Good resilience is an effective remedy for success. Failure should never be looked upon as the end of your journey but just a slight detour. Use failure to provide valuable lessons to make your journey the success it should be.

Accepting reality is the right route to moving forward. You need to be right where you are, be reminded that feeling discouraged is normal, and use it as a motivator to continue on track. Take deep breaths before plunging forward.

Take long leaps and bounds on your journey to success; strategize your next move in a positive direction. You should dismiss every cloud of denial and frustration. This is heavy, unnecessary baggage for you to take on your journey. You need to do as you are exhorted to do in **Hebrews 12:1, "Wherefore seeing we also are compassed about with so great a cloud of witnesses, let us lay aside every weight, and the sin which doth so easily beset us, and let us run with patience the race that is set before us." (KJV).** Make your decision fearlessly, and do not allow the two of the great enemies of success—fear and doubt—to let you say "No," "What ifs," "should haves," or "It could have." You should be able to reflect on why you do what you do, how you do what you do, and, more than all, what you must do. Examine carefully if your failure took you away from your "Why." If your answer is "yes," you need to address that immediately. Acknowledge the failure openly and honestly analyze what happened.

Reset your mindset, identify what motivates you, and try to keep that in mind when you are feeling doubtful. You can make smaller and more achievable goals; write them down if you must so you can see and track your progress. Obtain your lessons from your failures and mistakes, and journey with me on this interesting, rough, hard road leading to success.

Never opt to park on "Failure Ave." This is a dangerous street to be on. I must agree that failure is designed to crush your dreams and cast your ideas down the drain before they come to fruition. Instead, failure should be looked upon as an opportunity to improve. Our brains are wired to be more sensitive to failures and setbacks than successes; however, you need to maintain a strong perspective and not allow a few failures to overshadow the progress you have already made. Get up! Stand up! And continue your journey.

Chapter 2

Difficulties To be Encountered on the Road to Success

Many difficulties can be experienced on this road to success. Come along and take a walk with me on this amazing journey. We need to see and understand the possible hindrances that can prevent us from having a successful journey. The first hindrance is **fear.**

Fear can be the most difficult challenge that prevents you from achieving your objective. The dread of failure, the unknown, or the fear of achievement can be scary. Fear should not prevent you from progressing; it should be used as a tremendous motivation. If you are terrified of failing, you will be afraid of doing what you should do. Fear is simply the mind's way of indicating that you have something significant to gain control of. Never let fear stand in the way of success.

Emotional and mental incapacities are two more barriers to achievement. Like other pragmatic characteristics, these come naturally to some people but may be developed by anyone. To develop mental or emotional strengths, it is important to assess your perspectives on life and identify areas for improvement. This should be a moment for you to figure out what you want to keep and what you need to let go of. Setting gradual, reasonable goals is an effective way to create momentum and stay motivated. It is startling to notice certain circumstances that drag us down and cause us to lose focus, eventually allowing us to lose our direction.

Another strong barrier and opposition is **envy**. Envy prevents our safe journey to prosperity. It can be described as counting someone else's blessings rather than your own. You must pay attention and learn to appreciate what you have rather than what you do not have. No one else's achievement or fortune should prevent you from focusing and achieving your dreams.

The happier you are, the more successful you will become. Another person's success and fortune do not take away from yours. Be happy for someone who succeeds and concentrate on your abilities.

Let us examine another perilous and physically ridiculous aspect that can provide challenges on the path to success: **perfectionism.**

Perfectionism can be defined as a tendency to establish unrealistic standards for others. It is a dangerous and outrageous factor that can present difficulties on the road to success. Perfectionism can also be described as the inclination to set standards that are excessively high for us or others. Because of the unrealistic standards and goals set, many difficulties arise. It is inadvisable to cherish goals that only set us up for disaster.

Do not get this twisted; aim high and try not to tell yourself that you must be perfect in all you do. There should always be room for error. A perfectionist, unfortunately, always leaves what is to be done today for another day. This now leads to **procrastination.**

As mentioned earlier, when you become a perfectionist, you leave no room for error, which is super dangerous if you decide to finish this journey successfully.

It is also beneficial to leave room for constructive criticism. Perfectionists are always afraid of being criticized. Never be driven by fear; avoid becoming defensive when criticized, and stay strong and consistent.

Another factor that prevents smooth traveling on this road to success is **negative thinking.**

Negative thinking is useless because our minds are such powerful instruments. Anything you typically imagine becomes a reality. This method is well-known as a way of thinking. Sometimes, it seems so difficult that the possibilities begin to appear as impossibilities, and you begin to doubt your ability to succeed.

Negative thinking can be a highly risky setup for failure. As soon as you see these thoughts surfacing, replace them immediately with pleasant words and encouraging thoughts. Tell yourself, "I can do it. I have got this."

Let me draw your attention to another impediment to your successful trip on the road to success: **financial constraints**.

Financial constraints can be a significant barrier to making your journey successful and enjoyable.

When you do not have the money to do what you must do, completing a task is extremely hard. Some situations are hard or impossible to do if you cannot produce the money you need. Never be afraid of asking for help. It might be help from a friend, family, or anyone you can call for help. You might not succeed in getting the help you need; however, not seeking help should not be an option.

There is one crucial point I need to make: never forget to call upon God for help. He is our greatest helper. He is our Jehovah Jireh, our provider, who is always willing to help. **Philippians 4:19** states that God will supply every need according to His riches and glory in Christ Jesus. With God as our Father, Jehovah Jireh, our provider, we will not lack any good thing in life. Our God—our Father—has made the covenant with us that though the young lion does hunger and thirst, those who seek the Lord will never lack any good thing. We can hold on to God's promises when life's journey becomes hard and challenging. If you find yourself at a place you do not understand without provision, Jehovah Jireh, the Lord your provider, will give you what you need.

John 14:14 states, **"If you ask me anything in my name, I will do it."** Anything we ask for in prayer must be according to the character of God and in the will of God for it to be granted. Trusting Jehovah Jireh and embracing the confidence that He will supply our needs according to His riches in glory provides comfort to our souls. As He promises, we will never beg for bread; neither will our children and descendants beg for bread. He is faithful and will meet us at the point of our need.

While we exist here in life, it carries strong challenges; however, we should never be ready to admit defeat in a heartbeat.

Queenie Jones states, and I quote: *"When a task has just begun, never leave it till it's done. Be the labor great or small, do it well or not at all."* Mistakes are inevitable, but you should never look at your mistakes as defeat. Tough and challenging times will come, but you cannot give up before you see the positive results you anticipate.

Another boulder that you will find on this journey is **making excuses**. Set your goals and pursue them gracefully. Do not forget that times will come when the journey seems all uphill. It will look like you are running up a hill that has no end, but never become distracted. Keep your eyes fixed on your goal. Put your spiritual blinds on and maximize your level of determination. Do not make excuses; face your fears with aggression. Often, the things you are fearful of are sometimes things that have not yet happened and might never even happen.

Yet another thing can cause delays and defeats on this journey. What could this be? The answer is your **hobby.**

Hobbies are activities that are done regularly for enjoyment in life. Hobbies are fantastic, but they can keep you from reaching your God-given potential. Some people enjoy playing video games, wrestling, reading magazines, coloring, solving puzzles, watching Tic-Tok and videos, going on Facebook or Instagram, listening to music of their choosing, loading iTunes and Spotify, playing basketball, skating, etc. All of these are excellent practices or better described as hobbies. I am confident that each person will fit into one of the stated categories. Hobbies are nice to have, but there should be limitations. Some people let their passion or hobbies consume every moment of their time.

Free time is great, and it is necessary to maintain a balanced lifestyle; however, you should ensure your practice balances the activities. Arrange and distribute your time wisely. Set your goals and have a structure where you assign a specific time for each activity.

Another barrier that can present itself on this amazing road to success is **comparing yourself with others**. Comparing oneself is another hurdle and a major impediment on the path to success. Never try to compare yourself to anyone else. God spent time creating you; you are indeed special. Jehovah took the time to create you in His exact likeness, precisely as He wanted us to be. No matter how hard and long you search, you will never find a carbon copy of yourself. What an astounding fact! You were created to be unique. Your features are specially made for you; therefore, if you are a screw, do not attempt to be a nail; if you are a broom, do not try to be a mop. Would you put a stone on your plate instead of bread? You should endeavor to be the person God has called you to be.

Psalm 139:14 says, **"I praise you because I am fearfully and wonderfully made; your works are wonderful, I know that fully well." (NIV).**

The only person you cannot lie to is yourself. Difficulties are inevitable, but Doctor Bob Jones senior said, *"Make chariot wheels out of your difficulties and ride to success."* I am 100% certain that if every successful person should share their journey with you, it would be interesting to know that their success was only possible because they insisted on not giving up on this journey to success. One must pay attention to his/her goal. There is no need to compete with anyone. There should be no reason for you to look at someone else's success and think you must do what they did. Doing this will only create anxiety, stress, and, consequently, failure. It is okay to take tiny steps.

Never create unrealistic expectations while you are on your journey to success. Believe in yourself, even when no one else wants to. You cannot succeed if you fail to have self-confidence. Tell yourself, *"I'm unstoppable. I was born to succeed."* When you start doubting your ability, you are only creating negative beliefs in yourself that will prevent you from achieving your amazing success in life.

Everyone has weaknesses—some more than others—but create and exercise the ability to use your weaknesses as steppingstones to success. Take time to identify your weaknesses and work hard to eradicate them. If you can recognize or acknowledge them, this will be the initial step of overcoming them. Identify a person or person in your life who will be helpful to you and will assist you in overcoming the gray areas.

Please take note that there will be people who will be happy to see you fail; however, you will also find those who will assist you in any way possible to ensure that you make positive leaps and bounds. Stick to those people and learn to celebrate your success, even if it is you alone.

Here are some important things you need to do:

- Have a detailed rechargeable plan that states your goals.
- Divide the goals into smaller parts that are realistic.
- Pay attention to how you feel about the goals you set and intend to achieve.
- There are many difficulties in life, and it is okay to feel overwhelmed but never attempt to take on too much at once. As you are traveling along the path to success, you are required to make a lot of effort to reach your goals.
- Timing yourself appropriately and working minute by minute and day by day should be practiced.
- Never overthink or take on too much at once. Doing so may result in dissatisfaction and, ultimately, a catastrophic event. Continuous improvement and consistent advancement must be your guiding principle.
- It must be noted that many big and successful businesses typically began extremely tiny, sometimes in a one-bedroom apartment or on a back porch. Today, they own enormous establishments and are consistently progressive.
- Some companies may have begun in a simple basement; today, the sky remains the limit. I have met successful hair stylists

who told me they began with a single chair in their one-bedroom apartment. Today, they have grown to own amazing, fully operational, progressive businesses in prime locations. A few well-known store owners began their career peddling things out of the back of a vehicle; today, they emerge from behind the walls and are very forward-thinking, owning many chains of stores in various places.

- As you progress on this journey, examine your accomplishments daily and see if your journey is the way you intend to go. Ask yourself, "Is this journey leading me safely to the goals I have set?" If your answer is 'yes,' stay on your course. Never entertain the critics; stay positive, even when your strides are not that great, and remember that giving up is not on the list of your accomplishments.
- It is fine to talk to yourself and correct your actions and mistakes. Sometimes, you might even realize that your goals and actions might be conflicting. However, be mindful to avoid any form of putting off what you can do today for another day and keep the momentum going constantly.
- Use positive words and actions to correct your course. Find strength in weakness and learn to take risks. Striving for success and taking chances can take you out of your comfort zone. It is challenging, but it is a rewarding place to find yourself. This avenue is on the road to success, but the result of travelling there is great.

No real success comes easily. There must be struggles, fights, and even conflicts to achieve success. Chase your dreams passionately; that is all you are expected to do.

Here are a few interesting quotes that should serve as encouraging nuggets for you to digest:

"If you can dream it, you can do it, talk less, and demonstrate more actions." —Walk Disney

"There is a powerful driving force inside every human that once unleashed, can make any vision, any dream, and desire a reality." —Anthony Robbins

Believe in yourself; remember, a successful journey is designed for people who are willing to challenge what unsuccessful people are afraid to do. It is interesting to know that unsuccessful people never feel happy for successful people, but there is nothing sweeter than proving the procrastinators wrong.

Unsuccessful people will criticize you while you are in your pit; they will be happy to throw stones and debris at you, but the bricks and sticks of discouragement that are thrown at you and on you while you are down in that pit should be used to make a ladder to help you come out of your pit. Use them as steppingstones and watch yourself succeed right there in their faces.

It is a beautiful experience to watch God spread a gorgeous table in the presence of your enemies. To top it off, your enemies will be given front seats to watch you being blessed by God. God will make your enemies spectators and will even provide them with VIP seats so they can see the blessings of the Lord showered down on you.

Never, ever become sidetracked or distracted by the negativity of doubters. Know who you are and whose you are. Build your character from your experiences, tough times, sufferings, and victories. Put value on yourself, and remember, you are priceless. It is better to fail while trying than to give up and pretend you are succeeding. The journey to success requires a lot of effort and total dedication.

Another important ingredient that is needed for this journey is called **determination.**

Determination is a needed component for success to take place. We are God's prized possessions, and our walk should portray who we are. Practice determination; be dependent on the strength of the Holy Spirit and yield completely to God's will and His teaching of denying yourself of all filthy lusts.

Put determination in high speed and trod along. Be reminded that placing others before yourself is crucial to Christian living. The biblical meaning of "determination" goes far beyond willpower and self-motivation. It is rooted in a deep trust and total reliance on God's promises and guidance. Determination gives us the purpose of accomplishing God's goals in God's time, regardless of our opposition.

And let us not be weary in well doing for in due season we shall reap if we faint not. (Galatians 6:9 - KJV).

Determination is demanding work. Nehemiah turned the tide for God and his people. Nehemiah knew that despite the hardships and difficulties that stood before him, the God who was up in heaven was with him. The people were determined and had a mind to work. **Nehemiah 4:6** reinforces what we are talking about.

Determination keeps you moving forward. It is about staying absorbed in your goal. If you have a goal, you can easily create the path to that goal, moving even closer to the success you want. Certain benefits come with determination. I will try to list a few, so pay attention to these vital facts:

- Determination boosts creativity.

- Determination helps you to motivate others.
- Determination eradicates a feeling of hopefulness.
- Determination creates forward thinking.
- Determination builds positive thinking.
- Determination helps you to set lofty goals.
- Determination encourages perseverance.

Paul was a resolute individual who lived as an apostle of Jesus Christ. He was a fervent Pharisee and was notorious for his merciless pursuit of Christians to exact vengeance for their apostasy. Upon his conversion, we witness a man adamant about conducting God's will to the best of his abilities, regardless of the cost.

Og Mandino once said, *"If my determination to succeed is strong enough, failure will never overtake me."* It takes a lot of faith and belief to do anything. You should be resolute, totally committed, determined, hardworking, and have an unclouded vision. Recall that people who believe may not achieve anything, so remain mindful of what you already have. The less you focus on your needs, the happier you will be.

Remember that being flawless is not a goal. Thus, there is no need to move away from perfectionists but face them boldly. People on a successful journey need to be aware of perfectionism. You should never be afraid of what people think, nor be afraid of their judgment. Perfectionism is often associated with abuse in the highest order. It is never about trying to be the best. Instead, it allows you to be controlled by people's disapproval. Regrettably, some parents even set unrealistic, impossible, and unattainable ambitions for their children. This real issue should be called out when seen in action. Many kids become failures because of the unrealistic goals set by parents and other family members.

Look out for poor self-esteem—feeling that you are not good enough. Cultural and social expectations can sometimes play a negative role in perfectionism. It is always great to aim for the sky if you need to, but be careful that you do not allow this feeling to allow you to become so focused on trying to have everything in order, everything faultless, and no space for errors. This will land you in a dangerous zone and can negatively affect your life and aspirations. It can also affect your relationship with others and lead to bad emotional and social damage.

Do you recognize that you are being side-tracked by the feelings of having everything perfect? Rush to have this corrected immediately. How can this be done? How can this be corrected?

- Examine and readjust your goals.
- Listen to how you feel emotionally.
- Do not be afraid of mistakes and bad decisions you make.
- Relax in the oddest circumstances and tell yourself you are not defeated.
- If you sit with professionalism in your lap and start your pity party, you will be there nursing your failures. Eventually, you will find yourself on "Failure Avenue." Always strive to maintain a true balance and try to be less conscientious of your negative emotions.

It is important not to feed those thoughts and feelings and starve them. Do not apply fuel to the fire of perfectionism. All you will do in a case like this is set yourself ablaze.

The Word of God states in **Philippians 4:6-7**, **"Be careful for nothing; but in everything by prayer and supplication with thanksgiving let your requests be made known unto God. And the peace of God, which passeth all understanding, shall keep your hearts and minds through Christ Jesus." (KJV).**

The phrase **"be anxious for nothing"** is quoted so often in casual church talks that you will see it on book covers or hear your friends share such a thought. Some say that the phrase is written in the active tense in Greek, which implies an ongoing state. The apostle Paul wrote the book of Philippians during his imprisonment in Rome. He was exhorting the church in Philippi to follow his example. He encouraged them to speak the Word of God without fear when facing problems or persecution.

I sometimes doubt that we will go through life worry-free, but trusting in God requires a great deal of preparation. Being worried about nothing implies that we should be composed in any circumstance. We live in a chaotic environment where worry feels inevitable. The prison of anxiety is nonetheless genuinely voluntary. Paul wants us to know that we should never let anything in this world cause us to feel anxious. In the first place, even while we may experience worry, we do not have to be completely lost and buried in it. We do not have to completely immerse ourselves in our feelings of anxiety, even though it is feasible. The Bible provides clear guidelines on how to deal with anxiety. We can reduce our anxiety by praying, pleading for help, and expressing our gratitude to God whom we serve.

And we know that in all things God works for the good of those who love him, who have been called according to his purpose. (Romans 8:28 - NIV).

God gives us peace and hope. Nothing happens to us by chance; your life is in the comprehensive care of a faithful Father.

Chapter 3

A Glance at This Road to Success

The road to success is fascinating. What does the road to success look like? It can be challenging to respond to this question. I should pause for a moment to evaluate my trajectory and track in light of my 66 years of experience. I can tell you that it is challenging work to complete. From my vantage point, I believe that most people, if not everyone, aspire to succeed in life. The intriguing reality is that different people measure success in diverse ways. Everybody has a unique role to take. No measuring sticks, tapes, or other tools can unequivocally say "yes" to anyone that they have succeeded.

Some people have accomplished a lot in their careers, fulfilling their dreams of having the perfect job, house, spouse, and children, attending the most prestigious college or university, getting the highest degree possible, becoming extremely wealthy, owning the most luxurious vehicle on the market, all of which may enable them to live the cozy and fulfilled life they have always wanted. This is how they determine what constitutes their success.

The road to success is endless. There is always another turn, always another bend, always another mile or two to go. It is endless. When you think you have ended the path, you will realize you can keep on moving to higher heights and deeper depths.

When the road to success is examined, we should note that this road to success can be very tedious, and the only thing that can keep you going is your desire to succeed. This road is rough, rocky, and steep, with hills to climb, dark, lonely corners, bumps in the road, some rocky terrain, big tree roots, fallen trees in the way, big potholes, and areas where there is no light. You will also find enormous boulders that seem insurmountable. There are mountains to climb, and you will experience loneliness, hunger, lanes of disappointment, avenues of fear, destructive, dangerous pathways of doubt, and creeks of sicknesses of every kind. On this road, you will have tough nights as well as some bright sunny days. There are narrow, lonely paths of financial hardships, embarrassment, and very unfamiliar side roads with some reckless drivers and pedestrians threatening to knock you totally off track. You will encounter family, church, and relationship hurts. These are unavoidable paths to be found on the road to success. The beautiful consolation is that God has made every provision to keep you on track safely during these challenging times.

George A. Young was a carpenter by trade and a preacher who humbly served in small rural communities, often with small payments that resulted in hardship for his family. In his trying and challenging moments, he wrote this fitting song: *"In shady green pastures so rich and so free, God leads His dear children along. Where the waters cool flow bathes the weary one's feet, God leads His dear children along."* It goes on to say in the chorus: *"Some through the water, some through the flood, Some through the fire, but all through the blood. Some through great sorrow, but God gives a song, in the night season and all day long."*

Sometimes, we will find ourselves on the mountaintop, that place where the sun shines so bright; other times, we find ourselves in dark valleys with Satan opposing us on every hand, but by and through the grace of the almighty God, we fight the fight, and we will conquer through grace.

Knowing that God makes the necessary provisions for us to be victorious through any struggle is very comforting.

There are solutions that God has provided for your every need. Read and believe God's words; lean hard on His promises, and do not be alarmed when different emotions arise. There is a word from the Lord to strengthen you as you make your journey to success successful.

These are helpful nuggets to chew on when different emotions surface. I hope you will find them useful:

- **You are sad:**
  He gives power to the faint, and to him who has no might he increases strength. Even the youth shall faint and be weary, and the young men shall utterly fall, but they that wait upon the Lord shall renew their strength, they shall mount up with wings as eagles, they shall run and not be weary, and they shall walk and not faint. (Isaiah 40:29-31 – KJV).
- **You are afraid:**
  Do not be overcome by evil but overcome evil with good. (Romans 12:21 – NIV).
- **In despair:**
  Casting all your anxieties on him because he cares for you. (1 Peter 5:7 – NIV).
- **For consolation:**
  My peace I leave with you, my peace I give to you, not as the world gives, do I give to you, let not your heart be troubled, neither let it be afraid. (John 14:27 – KJV).
- **Courage:**

Finally, my brother be strong in the Lord and the power of His might. (Ephesians 6:10 - KJV).

- **You're sick:**
Lord, I know you are a loving God who hears me when I cry out to you, Father, please restore my health, just as your son had compassion for the afflicted, I ask you to pity me in my affliction, blessing me with the healing, I so long for. (Psalm 116:1-2 - NLT).

- **You are lonely:**
Fear not, for I am with you; Be not dismayed, for I am your God, I will strengthen you, I will help you, I will uphold you with my righteous right hand. (Isaiah 41:10 – ESV).

- **You are hungry:**
Come, all you who are thirsty, come to the waters; and you who have no money, come, buy and eat! Come, buy wine and milk without money and cost. Why spend money on what is not bread, and your labor on what does not satisfy? Listen to me, and eat what is good, and you will delight in the richest of good and let your soul delight itself in fatness. (Isaiah 55:1-2 – NIV).

- **You are timid:**
For God hath not given us the spirit of fear, but of power, and love, and a sound mind. (2 Timothy 1:7 – KJV).

- **You are rejected:**
The Lord is close to the brokenhearted and saves those who are crushed in spirit. The righteous person may have many troubles, but the Lord delivers him from them all; he protects all his bones, and not one of them will be broken. (Psalm 34:18-20 – NIV).

- **Peace:**
Do not be anxious about anything, but in every situation, by prayer and petition, with thanksgiving, present your requests to God. And the peace of God, which transcends all

understanding, will guard your hearts and your minds in Christ Jesus. (Philippians 4:6-7 – NIV).

- **Strength:**
Blessed is the one who perseveres under trial because, having stood the test, that person will receive the crown of life that the Lord has promised to those who love him. (James 1:12 – NIV).

- **When tempted:**
Let no one say when he is tempted, "I am being tempted by God," for God cannot be tempted with evil, and he tempts no one. But each person is tempted when he is lured and enticed by his desire. That desire when it has conceived gives birth to sin, and sin when it is fully grown brings forth death. Do not be deceived, my beloved brothers. Every good gift and every perfect gift is from above, coming down from the Father of lights, with whom there is no variation or shadow due to change. (James 1:13-17 - ESV).

- **Protection:**
He who dwells in the shelter of the Most High will abide in the shadow of the Almighty. I will say to the Lord, "My refuge and my fortress, my God, in whom I trust." For he will deliver you from the snare of the fowler and from the deadly pestilence. He will cover you with his pinions, and under his wings you will find refuge; his faithfulness is a shield and buckler. You will not fear the terror of the night, nor the arrow that flies by day, nor the pestilence that stalks in darkness, nor the destruction that wastes at noonday. A thousand may fall at your side, ten thousand at your right hand, but it will not come near you. You will only look with your eyes and see the recompense of the wicked. Because you have made the Lord your dwelling place—the Most High, who is my refuge—no evil shall be allowed to befall you, no plague come near your tent. For he will command his angels concerning you to guard you in all your ways. On their hands they will bear you up, lest you strike

your foot against a stone. You will tread on the lion and the adder; the young lion and the serpent you will trample underfoot. "Because he holds fast to me in love, I will deliver him; I will protect him, because he knows my name. When he calls to me, I will answer him; I will be with him in trouble; I will rescue him and honor him. With long life I will satisfy him and show him my salvation." (Psalm 91:1-16 – ESV).

- **Fear:**

The Lord is my shepherd. I lack nothing. He makes me lie down in green pastures; He leads me beside quiet waters, he refreshes my soul. He guides me along the right paths for his name's sake. Even though I walk through the darkest valley, I will fear no evil, for you are with me, your rod and your staff, they comfort me. You prepare a table for me, in the presence of my enemies. You anoint my head with oil, my cup overflows. Surely goodness and love will follow me all the days of my life, and I will dwell in the house of the Lord forever. (Psalm 23 – NIV).

- **Hard times:**

Cast your cares on the Lord, and He will sustain you. He will never let the righteous be shaken. (Psalm 55:22 – NIV).

- **Change:**

For I know the plans I have for you, declares the Lord. Plans to prosper you and not to harm you. Plans to give you hope and a future. (Jeremiah 29:11 – NLT).

- **Comfort when lonely:**

Do not fear, for I am with you. Do not be dismayed, for I am your God. I will strengthen you and help you, I will uphold you with my righteous right hand. (Isaiah 41:10 – NIV).

- **To be content:**

Let your conversation be without covetousness and be content with such things as ye have: for he hath said, I will never leave thee, nor forsake thee. So that we may boldly say, the Lord is my helper, and I will not fear what man shall do unto me. (Hebrews 13:5-6 – KJV).

- **Guidance when making decisions:**
  If any of you lacks wisdom you should ask God, who gives generously to all without finding fault, and it will be given to you. But when you ask, you must believe and not doubt, because the one who doubts is like a wave of the sea, blown and tossed by the wind. (James 1:5-6 – ESV).
- **Trust in God:**
  Trust in the Lord with all your heart and lean not on your own understanding. In all your ways, submit to him. And he will make your paths straight. (Proverbs 3:5-6 – KJV).
- **Protection in times of danger:**
  I will lift up mine eyes unto the hills, from whence cometh my help. My help cometh from the Lord, which made heaven and earth. He will not suffer thy foot to be moved: he that keepeth thee will not slumber. Behold, he that keepeth Israel shall neither slumber nor sleep. The Lord is thy keeper: the Lord is thy shade upon thy right hand. The sun shall not smite thee by day, nor the moon by night. The Lord shall preserve thee from all evil: he shall preserve thy soul. The Lord shall preserve thy going out and thy coming in from this time forth, and even for evermore. (Psalm 121:1-8 - KJV).
- **Finding a path to salvation:**
  Jesus answered, I am the way, the truth, and the life. No one comes to the Father except through me. (John 14:6 – KJV).

They replied, believe in the Lord Jesus and you will be saved you and your household. (Acts 16:31 – ESV).

If you declare with your mouth, that Jesus is Lord and believe in your heart that God raised him from the dead. You will be saved. (Romans 10:9 – KJV).

- **Finding forgiveness in times of conviction:**
Come now, let us settle the matter, says the Lord. Though your sins are like scarlet, they shall be as white as snow, though they are red as crimson they shall be like wool. (Isaiah 1:18 – NIV).

But if we walk in the light, as he is in the light, we have fellowship one with another, and the blood of Jesus Christ his son cleanseth us from all sin. If we say we have no sin, we deceive ourselves, and the truth is not in us. If we confess our sins, he is faithful and just to forgive us our sins, and to cleanse us from all unrighteousness. (1 John 1:7-9 – KJV).

- **Rest when weary:**
Come to me, all you who are weary and burdened, and I will give you rest. Take my yoke upon you and learn of me, for I am gentle and humble in heart, and you will find rest for your souls. (Matthew 11:28-29 – NIV).

Now these things occurred as examples to keep us from setting our hearts on evil things as they did. Do not be idolaters, as some of them were; as it is written: "The people sat down to eat and drink and got up to indulge in revelry." We should not commit sexual immorality, as some of them did—and in one day twenty-three thousand of them died. We should not test Christ, as some of them did—and were killed by snakes. And do not grumble, as some of them did—and were killed by the destroying angel. These things happened to them as examples and were written down as warnings for us, on whom the culmination of the ages has come. So, if you think you are standing firm, be careful that you don't fall! No temptation has overtaken you except what is common to mankind. And God is faithful; he will not let you be tempted beyond what you can bear. But when you are tempted, he will also provide a way out so that you can endure it. (1 Corinthians 10:6-13 – NIV).

- **Bereaved:**
  Blessed are those who mourn, for they will be comforted. (Matthew 5:4 – NIV).

  Praise be to the God and Father of our Lord Jesus Christ, the Father of compassion and the God of all comfort, who comforts us in all our troubles so that we can comfort those in any trouble with the comfort we ourselves receive from God. (2 Corinthians 1:3-4 – NIV).

- **Doubting:**
  Therefore, I tell you, do not worry about your life, what you will eat or drink; or about your body, what you will wear. Is life not more than food, and the body more than clothes? Look at the birds of the air; they do not sow or reap or store away in barns, and yet your heavenly Father feeds them. Are you not much more valuable than they? Can any one of you by worrying add a single hour to your life? And why do you worry about clothes? See how the flowers of the field grow. They do not labor or spin. Yet I tell you that not even Solomon in all his splendor was dressed like one of these. If that is how God clothes the grass of the field, which is here today and tomorrow is thrown into the fire, will he not much more clothe you—you of little faith? So do not worry, saying, 'What shall we eat?' or 'What shall we drink?' or 'What shall we wear?' For the pagans run after all these things, and your heavenly Father knows that you need them. But seek first his kingdom and his righteousness, and all these things will be given to you as well. Therefore, do not worry about tomorrow, for tomorrow will worry about itself. Each day has enough trouble of its own. (Matthew 6:25-34 – NIV).

Let us then approach God's throne of grace with confidence, so that we may receive mercy and find grace to help us in our time of need. (Hebrews 4:16 – NIV).

- **Healing:**
The Lord will keep you free from every disease. He will not inflict on you the horrible diseases you knew in Egypt, but he will inflict them on all who hate you. (Deuteronomy 7:15 – NIV).

I will bring health and healing to it. I will heal my people and let them enjoy abundant peace and security. (Jeremiah 33:6 – ESV).

People who let others dictate their beliefs should exercise caution because doing so might lead to a terrible and miserable outcome and often an empty life filled with anger, unfulfilled ambition, and ideas. Never hesitate to accept the result of your hard work. Always be ready for the worst, but at the same time, never give up. Acknowledge the result, no matter what it may be. One cannot enjoy life while facing obstacles. Obstacles will always stick their ugly heads in your attempts to achieve your objectives. They can occasionally be unforeseen; however, there is rarely a permanent detour or deviation.

"The real difficulty is to overcome how you think about yourself."
—Mayo Angelo

Always see yourself as the most beautiful, talented, and successful person existing. It is tempting to look at others and believe they are more progressive than you are, but this is often a big lie. Things are not always what they seem to be.

Keep believing in yourself, and remember you are a rare gem; you are exceptional. It is extremely easy to become a successful person. There are just a few things to put into practice and put in place if you desire to succeed. Stop for a moment and look at what you are today. See if this is what you want to be then. If you answer "no," ask yourself, *"Who did I want to become?"*

Set your goals and work towards achieving them. Today, you might look at yourself and think you are out of shape, weak, and sick, but start seeing yourself as strong, in shape, and healthy. Today, you might be so dissatisfied with your present situation or employment, but instead of grumbling and complaining, start working towards your dream job and push hard until you achieve it. Today, you might see yourself as uneducated, but instead of sitting down sobbing or crying, take classes to advance yourself and enhance your knowledge. At least try elevating yourself by reading a book a week and doing crossword puzzles. It is interesting to see how simple things can make a difference. Today, you might see yourself broke and utterly consumed in debt. Stop complaining and start working to become debt-free. Set goals and work to achieve them. Examine your plan to reach your goals. Put it on paper, write down the things you need to do and things to be implemented, and start working to achieve these goals. Stop seeing setbacks as difficulties and hindrances; stop throwing your arms up in the air and saying, *"I give up."* Instead, put your shoulder to the wheel and strive for excellence.

Remember that our aims and objectives should not be set on what we would like to do but on what we ought to do. The first "two" letters of the word **"goal"** spells **"go."** Remember, you are lost before you start if you have not figured out where you are going. Be encouraged as you continue this road to success.

Be a joyful pilgrim and not just a vagrant. A pilgrim can be described as one who is traveling to a certain place. A vagrant is a mere stroller with no settled purpose or goal. It may be a long way to reach a goal, but it is never far to the next step toward the goal. If you try and fail, do not stop. Keep trying until you succeed. Success involves persistence. Sacrifice involves persistence, failure, disappointment, hard work, discipline, and dedication. If you intend to become someone successful tomorrow, you must start today and be positive. Ask the oldest living person what his/her dreams and aspirations are. You would be amazed to find out that they still have many dreams and aspirations they have not yet achieved and would still love to achieve them if it were at all possible. Stop beating up on yourself for what you call underachieving. Instead, give thanks to God, who is still lending you breath, so you still have a chance to achieve.

As we said previously, this road to success can be measured differently by everyone. Some might find it easier to tell the story of their success than others, but never be timid about telling where you were and where you are today.

Chapter 4

A Mirror Synopsis Of My Journey

Reflecting on my own life, I can conclude that it has been a difficult trip on my journey to achieve success. I am still traveling and will try to provide you with a mirror overview of my life's adventure thus far.

The story told to me by my parents states that after having three boys, they were in serious prayer and supplication to God for a baby girl. Three years after my third brother was born, it was discovered that my mom was with child. Their trust in God was secure, and they believed by faith that the request of their hearts would be granted. They prayed, believed for a female child, and left it in God's hands.

After carrying me to full term, at precisely 8:00 am one gorgeous Sunday, February 22nd, 1959, Eulia Pearl McKoy and the late Reverend Dr. Alexander McKoy celebrated the birth of their first female child. This damsel was born a healthy eight-pounder, echoing a loud cry, allowing the sign of life to be evident as she entered this world.

The setting for this reality was a Nursing Home on Pryce Street in Kingston, Jamaica. Joyful tears of jubilation and delight filled the room and facility where I was born. My mother told me that when she was told that she had given birth to a girl, she instantly forgot all the anguish and suffering associated with childbirth. Shouts of jubilation, gratitude, and appreciation to God were heard because God answered their prayers. News spread like wildfire in the district of Point Hill, Saint Catherine, as they were informed that a damsel had joined the McKoy's army.

My mom and I were formerly freed as soon as we were cleared by the doctor and deemed well enough to go home. My lifelong record would include one remarkable response and significant information from the day of my birth. My birthday coincides with the birth of my parents' firstborn son, James, and two days after my dad's. How much more remarkable and God-designed could this be?

That Sunday morning, the sun shone brighter, heralding the arrival of a unique kid with a purpose on this planet. My dad joined us as soon as we were released from the Nursing Home. He was the happiest father and a trusted guide for us as we journeyed back to the hills of Point Hill, St. Catherine, where they lived.

My parents told me that I was wrapped securely in my mother's arms, ensuring I was kept safe as we journeyed in a chartered car on the bumpy winding roads. I was told as the car entered the neighborhood, people were seen at their gates watching out for my arrival.

As a minister of religion, my dad led two churches in that community, which made him very popular, loved, and respected, so his happiness would be the happiness of the community members as well. In those days, no one would be insulted or looked upon as being nosey by coming outside to witness my arrival. The air was charged with excitement as God fulfilled everyone's desire. The villagers were watching and snooping, ensuring they didn't miss a minute of the event.

Debrakay M. Brown

I learned my mom was so protective of me, so she cradled me to her breast so no part of me would be seen. All that was visible was a neat little bundle of joy held securely in her arms. Everyone looking on wanted to be a part of the eyewitness news that day.

To go fast forward, I grew and developed over the days, weeks, months, and years. My parents testified that they saw early signs of great intelligence, and my maturational age was significantly older than my chronological age. The community members would stop by regularly to get a glimpse of me. They would stand by the gate and watch me as I played outside and had fun making little comments. My only answer to them was, "I'm going to tell my daddy you troubled me." This amused them so much that they would have their party teasing me just to hear my repeated response.

From that early age, Dad was my protector, and he held that title until the day he passed at 93 years old.

My teachers were always proud of my achievements from preschool to kindergarten. I memorized lengthy poems and could recite the 66 books of the Bible without error. I was blessed with a terrific memory. My dad was transferred to oversee additional churches in other parts of the same Parish of St. Catherine, so our entire family moved to Ewarton, St. Catherine JWI.

At age nine, I encountered a close relationship with God. I attended a pre-New Year's Eve service at Ewarton Gospel Hall, St. Catherine JWI. After listening to the preaching, the late Rev. Edwards invited persons who felt the need to commit their lives to God to come forward. I did and was willing to make my decision to accept Him as my personal Savior. To date, I have never had a moment of regret.

Shortly after my conversion, my parents sent me to board right back in Point Hill, St. Catherine, because they wanted me to attend the renowned Point Hill Leased Primary School under the tutelage of the late Miss Latty, a phenomenal grade 6 teacher. She prepared me for the Common Entrance Examination that would give me a seat in a High School. I was indeed a successful candidate.

During my stay in Point Hill, I attended a sister church to the one where I was converted and was not short of Bible teaching. I was put in a class that prepared me for water baptism.

After a year of successful study, I was happy to go back home. On returning home, I went back to my home church, attended believers' classes for a few more weeks, and then had my baptism. In those days, ministers would make sure converts were certain of the vow they would be taking before baptism. Shortly after, my father's assignment changed again, so my entire family moved to Clarendon, where my dad was transferred to oversee a church that had failed miserably and needed urgent attention. Luckily for me, I gained admission to a renowned high school in the same parish.

During high school, I had a lot of interest in the sciences and started figuring out which professional role I wanted to pursue. As I matured, I became enthusiastic about nursing as a career. I spent my time in high school and did well on my external exams. Nearing the end of high school, I told my mom I wanted to study nursing in England when I graduated high school. My dream was to go to a University in England to pursue a nursing career; however, my mom did not agree with me going away from the care and love of my family to someone strange to take care of me. At that time, in my opinion, I believed my parents, especially my mom, were overprotective, but interestingly, I was just not the child to rebel against a decision made by my parents. I settled with the decision made. I then decided to work for a while, and while doing that, I would decide what my career move would be.

My first job was teaching at a commercial institution; teaching business, English, and Mathematics. The interesting thing was that after I accepted the offer and reported to work, I realized I would be instructing students who were even much older than I was. This made me a little nervous, but I was willing to take on the challenge.

I became enthusiastic about my work and was aware of the positive impact I was having on students' lives. My mother seized this chance to encourage me to become a teacher. My students were doing exceptionally well. I had to prepare twenty-two of them for their first external English and Mathematics examination. As a coach, I put myself in their lives, attempting to boost their self-esteem and instill confidence in them. When the examination finally came, all twenty-two students showed up for their English exam and eighteen for Mathematics. After a few weeks, the results were posted. They were as follows: 18 of 22 received honorary passes and 4 ordinary passes in English; for Mathematics, 18 sat the examination; 15 passed with honors, and 3 with ordinary passes. In the five years of that school's existence, they never had results like that. The principal and the school's governing board complimented and thanked me for the hard work and phenomenal results achieved. I immediately realized that the call on my life was much more than my little thoughts. It was evident that I had touched so many lives in a positive way in such a short time. This forced me to question, *"Is it God's will for me to become a teacher?"* I kept calm and watched God work things out in my favor.

Enrolling in Teachers' College was my next huge step, one that I embarked on willingly. The journey to get here wasn't straightforward, but it went well. There were moments of doubt, late nights, and challenges, but ultimately, it felt like a necessary part of my growth. I had worked hard to get accepted, navigating the application process and juggling other responsibilities, but the excitement of pursuing higher education kept me going. Once I arrived at college, everything moved fast.

The first few months were a whirlwind. There were new faces, different learning styles, and countless assignments. Some days, I felt overwhelmed trying to balance coursework and my personal life, but I always reminded myself why I was there: to become a better teacher and to make a real impact. As time passed, I found my rhythm, learning to prioritize and manage my time more effectively. I grew both as a student and individual, discovering more about myself and what I truly wanted from this experience. Now, with this semester drawing to a close, I was staring down my first final exam. It felt surreal. All the studying, sleepless nights, group projects, and long hours spent in the library had led up to that moment. It was nerve-wracking, but at the same time, I felt a sense of pride. My two majors in Teacher Education preparation were Religious Education and Music. So many things happened, but I distinctly recall that it was about time for my last practical musical assessment for the first year. I was called into the office of my Music Professor, who gave me specific instructions about a piece of music I needed to practice for my final examination. I was expecting her to give me the music sheet, but instead, she asked, "Debrakay, do you know the second-year student named Verniel Brown?" I reluctantly replied, "Yes, ma'am." According to my verbal expression and expression on my face, I knew she wondered why my response sounded that way; however, she never challenged my response but advised me to go to him and borrow a specific music sheet so I could rehearse for my finals. I reluctantly answered, "Okay ma'am." He was a senior student and, interestingly, one of the male students with whom I had never spoken. I knew he had seen me playing the piano at devotions, and he was a pianist because I also heard him playing at devotions. We just never spoke to each other.

I told my roommate, P, about the task I had to complete and asked her to go with me on this mission.

My roommate accompanied me to the entrance of the male dorm's staircase, which was the furthest we were permitted to go. I asked one of his batchmates to tell him that someone was downstairs to see him. He arrived soon after and was courteous and considerate. I made my request by giving him the message my professor gave me. He politely agreed, went back upstairs for the book, and handed it to me. I said, *"Thank you, sir,"* and promised to return it as soon as I was done. His answer was, *"My pleasure, young lady, no problem at all. I wish you all the best in your exam."* I felt like I had just removed a ton of bricks from my head, just getting the book without any lengthy conversation. This feeling towards him was not for any specific reason, but he was just not my friend.

I never saw him acting inappropriately as others did. He always portrayed himself as a dignified gentleman, and I suppose, thinking about the whole thing now, I can safely say he acted in a manner that fully explored the profundity of the heavenly mandate in his life. I would have to author a book three times the length of this one to tell half of my life's interesting love story, which continues healthily today.

After the exam, I returned the music book to him as agreed. He questioned me about my exam results, and I told him I was successful. He expressed how happy he was to hear of my success. It was now time for him to leave for his internship while I would go off for a holiday break and then return to the new round of my journey. Verniel was positioned at his new school and ready for an internship. I had no reason to even think about him.

Some weeks later, he tried to contact me. The weekend I left for home, he visited me at the college campus. Unfortunately for him, I was not there, so he left a message with the college nurse, stating that he had come to see me. On my return from my weekend break, I got that information and was surprised but did not read into it deeply. I just thought he wanted to discuss something related to music that he believed I could assist him with. Weeks later, one Sunday morning, while I was almost ready to go to church, I heard an announcement over the intercom that a visitor was in the lobby to see me. I was very startled because I had no idea who this visitor could be; I knew no one from the surrounding community. There was no way I could imagine that he would be the visitor. When I went to the lobby, I saw this gentleman smartly dressed in a chocolate brown suit, beige shirt, matching tie, and brown shoes. We greeted each other casually, but I only needed to find out why he was visiting me. I honestly thought he might have been visiting for something about music, so I waited patiently and anxiously for the question. He calmly but politely explained he was on a preaching assignment at a church in the area. He only stopped by to say hello to me and would return after he was done with his assignment to speak to me some more. At first, I thought that it was strange, but I left it as is. I spent a fleeting time speaking to him, and it would soon be time for me to leave for a Baptist church where I was invited to be a visiting organist that Sunday.

In the afternoon, after returning from church, I was called to the lobby to meet a visitor. There he was, waiting patiently in the lobby. His visit was very casual yet careful in his demeanor; the kind of visit that seemed innocent on the surface. We exchanged pleasantries, but I sensed an undercurrent of tension. As we settled into conversations, he subtly probed about my personal life, but his questions were framed as friendly curiosity. As we spoke, we both discovered that both our parents were ministers of religion. We shared similar religious beliefs, and we shared knowledge of other ministers who shared platforms between his assembly and mine. There was absolutely nothing I could hold on to during the duration of his stay to conclude the reason for this visit. He acted normal, very polite, respectful, and calm. He mentioned nothing that would cause me to believe he was in love with me either. Looking back, I can now say he was asking questions, waiting for clarity, torn between a desire to reveal his feelings and the fear of rejection if I turned out to be unavailable. Eventually, the visit wrapped up nicely. We parted without him even requesting a hug. We only shook hands and wished each other the best in our studies. I never knew that this guy's love for me was waiting in the shadows, hoping for a chance to step into the light.

Even now, when we reminisce, it still cracks me up when I remember that casual visit, just to find out much later that his intention for that visit was to try and figure out if the coast was clear enough for him to put in an application. Approximately one week after that visit, I received a letter in the mail from him. This was—and still is—the most shocking experience ever. It was a lengthy love letter that was intelligently penned and carefully worded, informing me of his love for me and his interest in pursuing a relationship.

I will never forget his opening statement in that letter. It read: *"Who can find a virtuous woman? For her price is far above rubies. Her husband doth safely trust in her so that he shall not need spoil. She will do him good and not evil in all the days of her life"* (see Proverbs 31).

He went on to say he sought God in prayer and fasting about this relationship, and God gave him the answer, which gave him the liberty to write to me. After reading the letter more than once, I felt somewhat confused because I wondered where and how this came about. I shared this with my dear friend, who was my adjoining roommate, that same P, and she was so amused by it but wished me well.

It took me a couple of weeks to reply, but I can clearly remember telling him in my reply that if he sought the Lord and got an answer, I would have to do the same before I could give any answer about it. I did mention to him that my Jesus and I had a good thing going, so I was persuaded that He would give me the perfect answer. I kept calm, prayed about it, and waited for my answer.

We arranged a meeting where we could meet face-to-face to discuss what this was all about and where we would be taking this. I still did not give him an answer at that time. I continued praying sincerely and waited patiently for God to give me the answer.

One interesting thing I want to share: I still have that proposal letter—forty-three years later—just in case I ever needed to remind him of all the grand promises he made. Honestly, though, I have never had to pull it out, and I don't think I will ever need to. He has been keeping up with his end of the deal extremely well.

I told my late dad, who was my best friend and confidant. I could tell and confide in my dad without an ounce of fear. I told him exactly what was going on and asked him to pray that God would order my steps in this decision. He cautioned me to take things slowly and carefully and encouraged me to rely on God to work things out in His own time; of course, he took it seriously and sought God for His divine will. He would check in with me periodically, saying, "Daughter, I am praying because I can't afford to see you hurt."

Eventually, I was satisfied that the answer came, and I felt confident about beginning a relationship with him. Shortly after receiving confirmation, I replied to his letter and consented to begin the journey.

The interesting part of this journey is when I realized the reason God shifted my plans. He had a special gift wrapped up in love, properly labeled for me. This gift was peculiarly fashioned in His likeness, strategically parceled, and tucked away in a safe place in that specific Teacher's College until it was time.

It is a formidable feeling to trust and depend on God's guidance. I can say that this is a profound aspect of faith that I find very comforting and transformative. When we trust God completely, it simply means that we surrender our desires and timelines, believing that God knows what is best for us. This trust in God can only lead to a deeper sense of peace and contentment, even amidst uncertainty.

When we open ourselves to His divine wisdom and seek God's direction through prayer and fasting, this can manifest unexpectedly through people, circumstances, or an inner sense of tranquility about a given decision. In these moments, we realize how God comes through for us, often at the right time, aligning our lives with His will and purpose. The patience required to wait on God is crucial, and waiting for God's timing can be challenging, but it teaches us resilience and deepens our trust and faith. Often, we may not understand why things unfold as they do, but hindsight can reveal the real beauty of His timing. Trusting God encourages us to embrace life's uncertainties with hope, knowing that He is guiding us every step of the way. When we are completely sold out to God and can trust His plan, it gives a very rewarding feeling.

I can recall that I never felt any need to get married. My feeling was to remain free, single, and disengaged. My desire was only to study and live a free single life with no marital commitment. That was not God's plan for my life.

As you can recall from my story earlier, this gentleman was my senior, and one of his majors was music. Interestingly, I was a junior, and one of my majors was music. The interesting thing was that my music professor was also his professor. This was a real setup from God.

I realized that God's will for my life was already tailored and properly mapped out. To make a long story short, on July 31st, 1982, I was joined in holy matrimony to the man God kept for me safely until it was time. He was indeed by God's design. July 31, 2025, will seal forty-three years of God's goodness, love, favor, kindness, and complete blessings and faithfulness in our lives. We have been blessed with two children, a king and a queen, and three amazing grandchildren who mean the world to us.

What a fascinating trip it seemed to have been from conception to different schools, moving on to higher learning, becoming a trained teacher, accomplishing other high academic achievements and accolades, becoming a wife, motherhood, and now a grandmother.

I need to reiterate without apology that the journey of every human being starts at conception. Joyfully or sadly, no two persons' experiences on this road to success are the same.

In the same way I encountered and wrote about my voyage without mentioning any challenging times, some people allow you to observe their lives with the idea that their lives are nothing but rubies and diamonds. I deliberately told you my tale the way I did to let you know that there are people who go on the same length to convince others that all that glitters is gold. That is far from the truth. That has never been proven to be true, not even once.

To sum up my story, I was born and raised a preacher's kid, and even though I was an adorable newborn that friends, relatives, and other community members had been waiting on for a long time—although they were all delighted to have me in their lives—I was still subject to all of life's hardships, challenges, difficulties, comforts, and pain. Being a pastor's kid, especially having a loved and exceedingly popular dad, only positioned me more into the public limelight and captured everyone's attention. My dad's name was spelled 'prominence,' and people would go out of their way to be around us. That did not always come off positively. Note that not all eyes were good and positive.

Some positioned themselves in certain ways only to search for any flaws. They often found something to point out and make fun of or to make mischief of. That alone made life extremely challenging for me. There were moments when I started thinking if some people were paid to take note of every move I made. It was evident and more than obvious that not everyone had the same motive, but as far as I was concerned, there were some unwelcomed and unqualified spies, people who could be given the fancy title of "Minister of People's Business" who dedicated their time to capturing every error I made. When some could not find an error, they created their own imaginary story, which sometimes looked and sounded as true as the words in the Bible. I am sure my siblings and other pastors' kids would share the same sentiments.

These encounters only stirred up resentment in me, and maybe people who meant me well were all packaged in my "no-fly zone bundle." They felt and seemed to be unwelcome characters who I kept a far distance from me. I started developing distrust and resentment for church members, irrespective of age, gender, and position in the church. I became very unfriendly and did not see the need to associate with people who, in my view, were just enemies.

It is incredibly sad to know that people seem to think that a pastor's child should be one innocent angel, perfect in all their ways. This situation would either make me or break me. I could never understand why we were expected to be exceptionally good kids and without blemish. It seemed like we were living in a different world from ordinary kids. That is how I felt for a long time. Many say up to this day that the pastor's child should even exhibit basic infantile habits. Nothing is farther from the truth.

As I became older, I understood that the older children who knew my family history and who I played with in school would go above and beyond to be considered my friend. I was granted certain advantages, including the constant right to first preference, and I was always given priority in secular and religious activities. Even during playtime at school, kids wanted to be in any game or group I was in. The main reason was that my dad's name made me famous, and kids wanted to be a part of the fame they thought I embraced. This did not always work out well for me because, as I said earlier, it always put me in the limelight.

Despite all that, I still had to deal with the realities of life. As I grew older, I edited the idea that life would not always be a bed of roses. Fairly early, I figured out that on my own, life's journey consisted of more than charmingly laid streets and well-mannered friends and acquaintances and that there were people who loved or hated me just because of my last name. There were incredibly significant obstacles in my life. You know, there have been times when events and situations happened to me that made me wonder if I was the same lovely baby that everyone wanted around. These times forced me to see and then realize how genuine and frail life is.

As I grew into a teenager, I saw how difficult life was for some of the girls my age and observed the bad choices some were forced to make because of people just sitting by and judging them. I was frequently left wondering how I would respond to some of the same situations or circumstances if I fell into a similar experience. Some fell on their faces because of needs, lack of support from family, and low self-esteem. Many lost focus or direction. I struggled secretly for a while to figure out my real interests, values, and even long-term goals. I grew up very sheltered, and although I did not need anything, I did not know the real world. I discovered for myself, without any clear purpose or direction, that the area of the brain responsible for risk assessment, judgment, and impulse control is still developing during our adolescent years. This mirror resulted in negative feelings, leading to choices and actions that may be considered dangerous and jeopardizing future opportunities. I was from a stable home, which was a plus. My late father could solve problems even in the direst circumstances and always found the bright side out of every dull moment. It was quite difficult to feel depressed in his presence.

I have always wondered how he managed to keep everything around him cheerful, so I could not identify or see the negative aspects of his existence. He helped me to stay focused and grounded, and I made it my goal to take some great qualities from him. My other siblings played a great part in helping me to develop good emotional intelligence, resilience, and life skills during my teenage years. We can be vulnerable to developing unhealthy coping skills at times, and this can sometimes lead to kids becoming depressed and anxious and can prevent a great child from succeeding at heart. I loved watching and mimicking my dad, and I realized from a young age how important it is to have caring adults who display a positive role model, guidance, encouragement, and examples for us to follow. As I said earlier, my father was all the above.

Teenage years are overly critical developmental periods, and the challenges faced during this time can have a long-lasting impact on a child's future trajectory. Although my family loved me, I still felt as if my life was paternalistic. I was never permitted to go out with friends, go on field trips at school, or participate in any secular activity. My life was sheltered. All my financial needs were met. I never experienced hunger, lack or shortage of clothing, or other personal needs, but I did not have the privilege or freedom to go out and play with friends and experience the real world. Only specially selected neighbors' kids would have the privilege of coming across to play with us in our yard, and this was only done under the watchful eyes of our mother. There were just one or two chosen neighbors' kids too. If they looked dirty, they were not allowed to play with us.

At that time, my siblings were four, Mom would say, *"You're five in number, so you're enough company for one another."* Life continued, but not without significant obstacles and challenges. There were times when life put me through its challenges, and I had to decide whether to let it break or make me.

There have been moments in my life when I had to face attempts to defile my character, even from those who seemed to hold high standing, including religious leaders and individuals who were well aware of my family background. In those moments, I was confronted with the choice of either remaining silent and letting my integrity be questioned or standing firm in who I am.

Though it was difficult, I chose to stand my ground. I refused to let their assumption or misjudgments define me. I spoke with clarity and conviction, asserting my worth and protecting my self-esteem. It was not just about defending my name; it was about holding on to my dignity and the values that define me, regardless of the titles or status others held.

In the end, standing firm in the face of their attempts to undermine me preserved my character and exposed their faults. I found strength in the truth of who I am and the lessons I have learned along the way. It was a powerful reminder that our dignity is something no one can take away without our permission.

My self-respect and strong Christian faith helped me get through some particularly challenging times and boring events. As a young child of eleven years, I enrolled in a private piano class. The love I developed for music contributed to my developing a positive mindset in several ways. Music helped me to develop emotional regulation. I loved listening to uplifting music, which elevated my mood and reduced stress. I always had my little CD player with my earphones in my ears. I would fall asleep at night with music playing. I was never exposed to outside events and pleasure, so music was my comfort. Listening to music helped me foster a more positive outlook on life. The upbeat and inspirational songs enhanced my motivation and encouraged my perseverance, driving me to my goal.

My experience listening to music conveyed a true message of love, empathy, and understanding. It helped me to appreciate others for who they are. Learning to play the piano and engaging in listening and playing pieces promoted mindfulness, allowing me to enjoy life more fully. As much as I loved music, I was still limited to the type of songs I could listen to or play because of my religious upbringing. Some songs were just forbidden.

After entering college and choosing music as my major, I was able to explore diverse genres; I broadened my perspective, fostering respect and appreciation for diverse cultures and people. It was there and then I realized that some of the same songs and lyrics I was not allowed to sing or listen to as a child had more meaning to life than some of the ones I grew up exposed to.

Music provided and still provides that creative outlet for my emotions and helped and still helps me process feelings and experiences, which led to great self-awareness and love for life. I practiced from that early age to integrate music into my daily routine as it helped me cultivate an incredibly positive mindset that propels me to achievements and enriches my relationships and overall appreciation for life and people in general.

I have had a strong passion for music over the years, and coupled with my being born into a musical family that deposited all the musical ability into me, my life became very fulfilled.

My late dad sang well and played the Hawaiian guitar skillfully. He taught my three brothers to play the guitar. My mother, even at the age of 94 years, is a great singer and coached the boys to sing while Dad taught them to play. My sister, who was born three years after me, is a guitarist and sings melodiously. My baby sister, who came thirteen years after the sister who followed me, is a great singer and plays the keyboard. There goes the entire McKoy family: talented musicians and singers.

To make this story more interesting, my only son plays the drums and the bass guitar professionally; my only daughter sings extremely well and is musically literate; my oldest grandchild plays the violin; my middle granddaughter plays the bass guitar, and my only grandson plays the saxophone. As mentioned earlier, my hubby is a music major who plays the keyboard, is an accordionist, and can sing any part of a song, including soprano, alto, tenor, and bass if he needs to. He was also born into a music-literate family.

When God sets you on the journey to success, relax and trust His guidance. Trust the process. God certainly knows how to supply our needs, and once we seek Him first, He instructs us on what to do. He is a real promise-keeper.

Debrakay M. Brown

Life has shown me the different turns it can take; some of the lanes, avenues, and streets were sometimes scary enough that it would have led me to total catastrophe, but because my faith and confidence in Jehovah was unwavering, my walk has been challenging at times, but remarkably successful.

My marriage has been great years, certainly not free of challenges, barriers, weird boundaries, bumps in the road, crooked lanes, demanding circumstances, dark rivers, and rocky terrains but to God be the glory. All these experiences have planted my feet on solid ground. We have never lost hope, neither love nor respect for each other. God has allowed our lives to be outstanding examples to our kids, grandkids, and innumerable people who have crossed our paths. Both of us now constantly remind each other of the miraculous way God prepared us and put us together for life.

My husband is incredible, embodying strength and compassion in every aspect of his life. As a blessed and responsible man of the cloth, he not only supervised the spiritual needs of seven churches in the Caribbean but also served as a marriage officer whose license put him at liberty to perform marriage ceremonies in the fourteen parishes of Jamaica. He has been privileged to guide countless couples through their journey. His dynamic preaching resonates with many, displaying his powerful faith and ability to connect with others. He has ministered in countries like Grand Cayman, England, Bermuda, Canada, and several states in the United States of America. As a father of two biological children and a loving grandfather to three, he demonstrates the essence of family, providing support and love.

His role as an amazing brother and adoptive father to many speaks to his generous heart. Despite his firm commitment to his beliefs, he maintains an easygoing demeanor, making him approachable and relatable. His culinary skills add a special touch to family gatherings, and his humanity and straightforward nature make him a respected leader and a trusted friend. His love for God and his family is the foundation of his life, making him a remarkable husband and a beacon of light in many lives.

God has kept us safely, and we will never let go. I keep climbing over every barrier, defying the odds, picking myself up from the rubble, brushing myself off, and continuing my road to success. I have become a teacher, wife, mother, friend, acquaintance, counselor and advocate, musician, good cook, baker, entrepreneur, leader, comedian, an undefeated champion of love, a devil chaser, acquired leader, young people's director, Sunday School teacher, Sunday School superintendent, young people's and woman's federation president, choir director, both senior and junior choirs, songwriter, and writer of innumerable poems waiting to be published. I have worked in the capacity of principal and founder of my first commercial institution, where I was able to cater to boys and girls who failed their high school years and were given another chance to make their lives worthwhile. I was the founder and director of three day care centers for fifteen years in the United States, a mother, grandmother, aunt, sister, godmother, woman of faith, prayer warrior, sister-in-law, voice for the less fortunate, promise, possibility, a very big bundle of potentiality, to name a few. More than all the above mentioned, I am born again, a blood-washed, humble, but powerful woman of God; a no-nonsense force to be reckoned with.

Every morning, as I wake up and my feet hit the ground, this very act signals a powerful shift. I embody potential and purpose daily, and this degree of purpose shows the devil and his angels the degree of light I carry with me. He trembles at this awakening, knowing that every step I take toward my goal and values undermines his influence. I aim to stay humble and never try to exalt myself in any way. I know my name is '**Purpose**' and purpose never dies.

Debrakay M. Brown

I have come to know the undeniable call of God on my life, a call that transcends the opinions of others and the barriers they may attempt to place in my path. God has instilled a unique purpose in me, and I refuse to let anyone or any institution stand in the way of fulfilling the mandate He has given me.

Though the journey has not been easy, I am resolved and will not sit idly by or allow myself to become stagnant. I am determined to keep moving forward, led by God's guidance, knowing that His plan for me is greater than any challenge I may face. Through His strength, I find the courage to overcome obstacles and take bold steps in fulfilling my calling.

Writing this my first book is a step in that journey—a tangible way for me to share God's goodness and use the gifts He has given me to impact others. I know that the road to success is not without hardships, but I am certain with God's hand upon me, every challenge is an opportunity for growth and a reminder of His faithfulness. As I press on, I am committed to staying true to the vision God has placed in my heart, confident that He will lead me through every trial and bring me to the fulfillment of His purpose for my life. My determination to choose goodness, spread kindness, and pursue my true path creates a significant ripple effect that disrupts the darkness no matter how thick it is.

When I think of even how my body fights the challenge of neuropathy pains in my feet, especially at night, I am blessed to know that the grace and strength of God allow me to get out of my bed and transform into a bold declaration of resilience, shaking the very foundation of fear and despair. In these moments, I spare no effort to assert strength and defy the shadows of bodily aches and pains that sometimes try to hold me back. The devil trembles to see that God continuously orders my steps.

I am blessed to have touched countless lives in extremely positive ways. The crux of the matter is that I switched professions, but I matured and realized that this was what God wanted me to do. I can refer to God's Word in **Psalm 119:105,** which states: *"Your word is a lamp for my feet, a light on my path." (NIV).* I can say with confidence, "Nothing happens to me by chance."

Proverbs 3:5-6 encourages us to trust in the Lord with all our hearts; acknowledge Him in all our ways, and He will make our paths straight. **Psalm 32:8** states: *"I will instruct you and teach you in the way you should go; I will counsel you with my loving eye on you." (NIV).* **Isaiah 30:21** states: *"Whether you turn to the right or to the left, your ears will hear a voice behind you, saying, "This is the way; walk in it." (NIV).* **Jeremiah 29:11** states, *"For I know the plans I have for you,"* declares the Lord, *"plans to prosper you and not to harm you, plans to give you hope and a future." (NIV).*

It is truly amazing the lives I have touched on this journey. My life is a living testament to the power and magnitude of a big God. Many lives have been changed and rearranged, and all the glory and praise go to almighty God. God has blessed me in many ways, and it has been proven that He has everything about my life organized. I have become a beacon of light and hope with unwavering faith, which always propels me to ride out my storms and accomplish my dreams. My battles are too many to number, and although they have been severe, they have not worn me down; giving up was never an option because I never lost hope.

I remember coming upon boulders indicating this was the end of my victory, but I did not take the bait. I looked the devil straight in his face and let him know he was a father of lies, and I was aware of his tactics. I have encountered unsurmountable challenges of all kinds: physical, emotional, and spiritual. I have asked why dreadful things happen to good people. I am sure this is not frightening or strange to any true believer determined to finish the journey successfully. Remember, God created us and knew us from our conception. He allows certain things to happen so we can grow and become more like Him. The experiences we face and the struggles we encounter help us learn how to trust in God.

You might sometimes feel He does not care about you, but it is the opposite. He loves us enough to know that whatever He allows to happen will help us to fulfill our divine potential as His children. Sometimes, the situations that we face seem all-consuming, but we serve a big God who cares about us.

Many things in life sometimes seem questionable, but as Confucius says, *"It does not matter how slowly you go, as long as you do not stop."* You need to make this affirmation daily.

Obstacles are designed to stop you, but you do not have to stop. You might find yourself running into some big giant walls, but if that happens, do not stop or put your hand in the air and give up. Stay right there and try to figure out a way to climb over or even through the barriers. These obstacles can be scary, but keep your eyes on your goal in the toughest times. As long as life exists, you must face challenges. Challenges are portals that are inevitable; however, defeat is by choice. Your responsibility is to take things one step at a time. When you see how the wind and the storm beat against the trees, you will see that some trees take the beating and get stronger.

Some storms help us to determine how strong we are. Some people in a marriage partnership become quickly frustrated in the early stage. You must remember that two strangers fell in love under God's sacred law, struck a deal, united, and joined in holy matrimony. Some individuals who come together are unaware of each other's genuine preferences and dislikes, and unfortunately, other nasty behaviors begin to surface after the union begins. At this time, when an individual starts displaying their authenticity, it does not mean you should pick up your belongings, grab hold of your feet, and flee. This is a time you should send your roots down deeper, try to survive the wind, and prove what you are truly made of.

I am no exception to marital challenges. I have had experiences, frightening ordeals, things I was never used to, and situations where I forgot the oath of submission as a wife just because my ego dictated to the contrary. That weird voice told me that I was my own big woman; I collected my paycheck, I was an adult and, therefore, I should be able to make whatever decisions I wanted to make without being compelled to do what I didn't think necessary. This behavior happens on both sides when my husband thinks this is what must be done, and neither of us refuses to take the lower seat. That is a big problem. If success is expected, someone must be willing to take the lower seat on this journey. A very interesting strategy of our relationship is that no matter what transpires, we never lose respect for each other and are always willing to apologize in a heartbeat. This is a pledge we made before marriage; respect and love for each other is one of the foundation columns supporting and undergirding our relationship. This is the fastest working medicine and remedy for marital ailments. It works like a charm. It does not mean that doing what is wrong deliberately every time and saying you are sorry quickly should be a constant habit. When you do something wrong and say you are sorry, a special effort should be made not to repeat the same mistake over and over; this will cause mistrust.

My road to success has been rough but successful. God has put us together for life and has remained faithful to us through the battles, pitfalls, and victories won. I have been knocked down but never knocked out. I kept climbing over every barrier, defying the odds. I face my fears aggressively and have discovered that the things I often fear, like failure, rejection, and uncertainty, can become stepping stones to success. These challenges push us to grow, develop resilience, and discover new ways to overcome obstacles. Each setback teaches valuable lessons that build strength and perseverance. Embracing fear as a learning experience rather than something to avoid can open doors to unexpected opportunities and personal growth.

I am enjoying my interesting, challenging, yet successful journey on this road to success paved with hardships.

Chapter 5

A Faithful God

The challenges of life have hardened, molded, and made me strong. All the experiences I had caused me to evolve into a great woman. Today, I can proclaim, *"I will always be the victor."*

I have experienced some major miracles in my life. I remember suffering from severe and constant migraine headaches for many years. I would be knocked down numerous times from unbearable migraine attacks. I can recall being hospitalized for two weeks, doing all sorts of tests and brain scans, trying to find out the cause of the painful, unstoppable headaches. I can remember being discharged from the hospital with less pain after two weeks, but not completely delivered from the attacks. I went to the church where my late father ministered and supervised; I sat around the organ because I was the organist then. My dad asked congregants to join him in prayer and believe in God for divine healing from this debilitating migraine headache.

Deacon B (now deceased) was asked to lay his hand on me while the church interceded, prayed over me, and believed God for a miracle. Deacon B placed his hand directly on my head and prayed for my divine healing. Thanks be to God; this prayer was answered. The headaches started to be less and less severe until they disappeared.

After relief for many years, I migrated to the United States of America, and shortly after, the migraines returned with a vengeance. Fervent prayers were offered again for divine healing. Twenty-two years to this date, I have been migraine-free. I do not know what a simple headache feels like anymore. To God be the glory.

Anyone reading this testimony suffering from migraine headaches or other sicknesses, be encouraged; no matter how impossible things seem, keep trusting God for your deliverance. If He did it for me, He will do it for you. *"If you trust God, do not worry, and if you worry, don't trust Him."* Those were the exact words of my late dad to me.

Another memorable miracle was when God healed me from kidney stones. One day, I started having very excruciating pain in my lower back with terrible pressure on my lower abdomen. The flow of my urine was interrupted, so I rushed to my doctor. He sent me to do tests that confirmed I had a kidney stone. He prescribed medication and decided that he would wait a few days to see if I passed the stone on my own before considering doing surgery. He instructed me to drink copious amounts of water and hope for the best.

I went home feeling very despondent and still in pain. I remember clearly that, as I got home, I went straight to my late dad, who was a strong believer in divine healing. I explained to him my situation. He called me closer to him, laid his hands on the area that hurt, and prayed. This was his exact prayer: *"Lord, I'm presenting my child in Your hands. I curse any surgical knife that would be placed to operate on this, my offspring. I claim a miracle now. Kidney stone, I command you to be flushed out, in Jesus' name. Give her a divine miracle with signs following so we can all see the evidence to confirm her deliverance, in the name of Jesus."* At that moment, I said, "Amen," but I didn't fully understand what it was to use my faith to believe in my deliverance. I was relying on my father's faith to work on my behalf. That is as much as I understood at that time because I was so consumed in pain.

The following day, I felt an urgency to urinate. The pain I was feeling was tripled. I rushed to the restroom, and as I sat on the toilet, I started having unbearable, excruciating abdominal pains that forced me to yell at the top of my lungs. I wanted to urinate so badly, but I had trouble doing so. While going through that ordeal, I got a release, and just before the release came, I felt and heard when something fell in the toilet bowl. I distinctly heard a 'ping' sound. I was so nervous. Finally, the pain came to a sudden end. I was surprised when I looked into the bowl; I saw the stone at the bottom of the bowl. I was crying aloud, astonished. I called my mom and dad to see the stone I passed in the toilet. My mom put a glove on and took the stone out so I could have it as proof. This was the sign my dad asked God as proof of deliverance. I was able to bring the stone to my surgeon, who was also my PC, and showed him what had happened. He admitted that that was indeed an act of God. God intervened peculiarly on my behalf.

There are too many more deliverances of healing that I have experienced while on this road to success. The devil is aware of the blessing I am and the blessing I will be, so he works overtime to attack my health in so many ways and so many unconventional times. The good news is that I know who I am, and I also know who has my life in his hands, so I keep lifting myself and moving forward. The storms of life come dashing so many times. The tempests have been wild on sea and land, but I resort to seeking my places of refuge in the hallow of God's almighty hands. Sometimes, there seems to be no hope, but in those moments, the reassuring, still, small voice whispers, *"I am with you, My child."*

There are innumerable times when I could have given up, admitted defeat, held both hands up, and cried, *"I surrender to the plots of the enemy,"* but *"No way!"* I continue to stand my ground, withstand the tests, and win the battles. I have been hit many times by boulders, large stones, hot bricks, and sticks, stumbling over traps in my path but I never stayed down. In these moments, I hear the voice of my savior forcibly in my ears, saying, *"My child, I'm right here with you. I will hide you safely, hide you where no can e'er betide you, I will hide you safely, hide you in the shadow of My hands."*

There have been times when different afflictions plagued my body; they came to weaken my steps on the journey, but in love, God quickly came to my rescue and lifted me above the attacks. Despite the battles and innumerable attacks of the enemy on this road to success, I continue to bear the cross of Christ with extraordinary pride. I have faced some serious storms and wild billows, but while all of this is taking place, God cares for my soul, and nothing can harm me as His child.

The greatest glory in living is not in failing but in rising every time you fail. Just remember that setbacks and challenges are a normal part of life. Luckily, the best happiness is to push ahead and reshape your mindset as you fall.

Stress can take a serious toll on your body, so in every circumstance, try to cultivate joy in your life so you can keep pushing through challenging times and look forward to better days. Feeling unmotivated or uninspired can deplete your life of happiness and meaning, but it is all about perspective. Keeping hope alive in the face of adversity is one of the most powerful acts of resilience we can practice. When life feels overwhelming and circumstances seem bleak, never lose sight of the possibility of a change or improvement and keep hope alive. Hope is a choice that requires nurturing even in the darkest moments. To keep hope alive, we must acknowledge that while we don't always have control over what happens around us, we have the power to choose how we respond. Shifting our focus from what is out of our control to what is within our reach helps us maintain a sense of hope. Hope doesn't require blind optimism; it asks us to look for small rays of light amid darkness, no matter how faint.

The heat will be turned up to a degree that will seem far beyond normal with no sign of relief. I have had moments on this journey where people I deemed to be my friends were nowhere to be found. The people I helped and ministered to, helped out of distressing and disastrous circumstances; the people I fed when they had nothing to eat, put clothes on their backs, comforted when their own treated them like dirt; people I took in my home and nurtured back to health were the ones who turned around, betrayed me and behaved like they didn't even know me. I have had close family members act as if I was never born. It was unbelievable to see who hurled the biggest rocks at me; they were loved ones I depended on, those I called my own. I looked to them to have my back; those were the ones who provided the weapon to stab me in my back and the bullets to destroy me. I am so happy God gave me the courage and strength to forgive them.

The Word of God says in **Psalm 27:2-3,** *"When the wicked advance against me to devour me, it is my enemies and my foes who will stumble and fall. Though an army besieges me, my heart will not fear; though a war breaks out against me, even then I will be confident." (NIV).* **Isaiah 41:10** says, *"So do not fear, for I am with you; do not be dismayed, for I am your God. I will strengthen you and help you; I will uphold you with my righteous right hand. (NIV).* We have no reason to fear because God promises to protect us from the hands of the enemy. It doesn't matter how we feel or how the circumstances present themselves; we have the promise of a covenant-keeping God who will remain true to His Word. He is not slack concerning His promises.

Isaiah 41:10 is a direct message from God to us as His children, but especially to those who are afraid. When we examine the verse, we must look at God's redemption plan for the exile remnants of Israel. God made a promise to bring out the chosen offspring from bondage to a promised land. God encouraged Israel to put their trust in Him despite their past rebellion. God did not abandon Israel through their long journey from slavery in Egypt. God wanted His people to understand that He has always been and will always stay with them. He was still their God who would keep His promise to help them.

God's promise to strengthen you goes much deeper than on the surface. In the original Hebrew, the verb translated *strength* entails making someone stronger and stronger. It means to grow, develop, prevail, and have or show courage to seize, grasp, and keep. God knew of the weaknesses of His people; He therefore used everything in their personal experience and journey of faith to develop courage and strength in them. The Lord was with them. He had seized hold of them and would never let them go no matter how hard the journey seemed.

God strengthens and preserves. He serves as a piloting hand; God's right hand symbolizes His power and strength. The Lord's presence with us and our unwavering trust and faith in Him results in our strength. God supplies power to the weak and strength to those without power; even youths will become weak and tired, and young men fall in exhaustion, but those who trust in the Lord will be renewed in strength. They will soar high on the wings like eagles. They will run and not grow weary; they will walk and not faint because of their close relationship with God. The Psalmist says, *"My health may fail, and my spirit may grow weak, but God remains the strength of my heart." (Psalm 73:26).* He is mine forever; the same inspiring power of God demonstrated throughout Israel's history is still available to us today.

We can make our journey successful through a close relationship with Jesus Christ. No matter what we face on this journey to success, we have hope. If we are born of God's Spirit, Jesus becomes our total source of strength, and we will be able to overcome all the difficulties, trials, and temptations we encounter on this interesting journey. The apostle Paul testifies that it was God's strength alone that enabled him to preach the gospel. Paul said, *"But the Lord stood at my side and gave me strength so that through me the message might be fully proclaimed, and all the Gentiles might hear it. And I was delivered from the lion's mouth. The Lord will rescue me from every evil attack and will bring me safely to his heavenly kingdom. To him be glory forever and ever. Amen." (2 Timothy 4:17–18 - NIV).* Paul trusted God, who stood at his side to give him strength and deliver him safely through every hostile experience until he reached his heavenly home. God used Israel's personal experience of adversity and hardship to strengthen them. He uses our suffering today to prove Himself to us. Peter wrote that in His kindness, God called you to serve and share in His eternal glory through Christ Jesus. After you have suffered a little while, He will restore, support, sustain, and strengthen you, and you will be placed on a firm foundation. James also taught that our suffering produces strength and character.

James 1:3-4 states that there will someday be strong believers who will feel the way the Israelites felt while they were in captivity: abandoned, rejected, totally disheartened, alone, and afraid. If you need God's strength today, remember it is comforting to hear Him say, *"Fear not, for I am with you; Be not dismayed, for I am your God. I will strengthen you, yes, I will help you, I will uphold you with My righteous right hand." (Isaiah 41:10 - NKJV).* Thank God for His constant reminder and willingness to be our aid as we journey on this path to success.

This journey is endless. There is always another way. When you think you are close to the end of a lane, you often find out your journey is still in progress. This journey's limit is the sky. According to your vision for this journey, you will discover that there are higher heights and deeper depths to travel.

There are persons we have read about in the Bible who experienced challenges on this road to success filled with hardships. Some undoubtedly experienced awful situations and unbelievable circumstances. Sometimes they were even knocked to the ground, but with perseverance and trust in God, their journey ended successfully.

Chapter 6

Trials to Triumph

JOSEPH, THE DREAMER

Joseph's journey from trial to triumph is a story that unfolds with a deep twist of betrayal, hardship, faith, and ultimate victory that has been related in the book of Genesis. Joseph, the 11th son of Jacob and the firstborn of Rachael, was loved dearly by his father. The favoritism caused great resentment among his ten older brothers, who grew jealous. One day, when Joseph was sent to check on his brothers while they attended the flock, they conspired to kill him. However, Reuben, the eldest, suggested that they throw him in a pit instead. Later, they decided to sell him to a passing caravan of Ishmaelites who took him to Egypt. In Egypt, Joseph was sold to Potiphar, an officer of Pharaoh. Joseph thrived in Potiphar's house, gaining his master's trust. However, Potiphar's wife falsely accused him of attempting to seduce her after he resisted her advances. As a result, Joseph was thrown in prison.

Despite his wrongful imprisonment, Joseph maintained his faith in God. While in prison, he earned the favor of the prison warden and interpreted the dreams of two fellow prisoners, a cupbearer and a baker, both of whom had been imprisoned by Pharaoh. Joseph's interpretation of the dreams came true, the cupbearer was restored to his position, and the baker was executed.

Two years later, Pharaoh had a troubling dream that none of his advisers could interpret. The cupbearer remembered Joseph, and he was summoned to interpret the dream. Through God's guidance, Joseph interpreted Pharaoh's dream to mean that Egypt would experience seven years of abundance followed by seven years of famine. Joseph advised him to store grain during the years of abundance to prepare for the famine. Impressed by his wisdom, favor was shown to Joseph. He was appointed second in command over all of Egypt and was responsible for managing the grain stores.

During the famine, Joseph's brothers, who were struggling in Canaan, came to Egypt. Taking food, they did not recognize Joseph, who had risen to power. After a series of tests, Joseph revealed his identity to his brothers, and despite their earlier betrayal, he forgave them. He invited them to bring their father, Jacob, and their family to Egypt, where they were given land to settle. This story is one of remarkable faith and resilience. These trials: being betrayed by his family, sold into slavery, falsely accused, and imprisoned, were all stepping stones to his eventual triumph. Through it all, Joseph trusted in God's plan for him. In the end, Joseph rose to power and saved Egypt from famine, and reconciled his family, fulfilling God's promise to Abraham that his descendants would be a great nation.

And God sent me before you to preserve a posterity for you in the earth, and to save your lives by a great deliverance. So now it was not you who sent me here, but God; and He has made me a father to Pharaoh, and lord of all his house, and a ruler throughout all the land of Egypt. (Genesis 45:7-8 – NKJV).

In the same way He brought out Joseph, God's favor returns to us in places and ways we least expect. As long as we remain faithful to God, He will come through for us.

MOSES, THE DELIVERER

Moses' journey with the Israelites was a pivotal narrative in the Bible, primarily found in the books of Exodus, Leviticus, Numbers, and Deuteronomy. After the Israelites came out of slavery in Egypt, Moses faced numerous challenges in guiding them through the wilderness. His journey was marked by trials, including conflicts and doubts among the people. Despite these hardships, Moses remained a steadfast leader, frequently turning to God for guidance. The key events included the Ten Commandments on Mount Sinia, which established the covenant between God and Israel.

Throughout the forty years of wandering, Moses taught the people about faith, obedience, and community. Though he led them to the borders of the promised land, he was not allowed to enter it himself, so he passed leadership to Joshua. The transaction underscored Moses' role as a prophet and leader; he ensured the continuation of God's promise to the Israelites.

Moses had so many struggles on his journey that he would make any leader give up. Moses had many internal battles, but he persevered and believed in God. He encouraged the people not to be afraid but to stand still and wait for the Lord's rescue.

And Moses said to the people, "Do not be afraid. Stand still, and see the salvation of the Lord, which He will accomplish for you today. For the Egyptians whom you see today, you shall see again no more forever. The Lord will fight for you, and you shall hold your peace." And the Lord said to Moses, "Why do you cry to Me? Tell the children of Israel to go forward." (Exodus 14:13-15 – NKJV).

No matter what we encounter on this journey, we need to exercise perseverance. Moses displayed perseverance and reminded us to call on God for help when the challenges seem unsurmountable.

RUTH, THE LOYAL WOMAN

Ruth's story is one of loyalty, faith, and divine providence. Ruth, a Moabite widow, chose to stay with her mother-in-law, Naomi, after the death of her husband, instead of returning to her people. This act of devotion led her to Bethlehem, where she gleaned in the field of a wealthy landowner named Boaz. Boaz was impressed by Ruth's commitment to Naomi and eventually married her, securing her future and legacy. Ruth's trial was not only her loss but also the societal challenges of being a foreigner and widow. Her triumph came through her unwavering faith and hard work, and her marriage to Boaz restored her family's name and position. Ruth became the great-grandmother of King David, which highlighted the significance of her story in the lineage of Israel's monarchy, showing how faithfulness and trust in God can lead to unexpected blessings.

But Ruth said: "Entreat me not to leave you, or to turn back from following after you; for wherever you go, I will go; and wherever you lodge, I will lodge; Your people shall be my people, and your God, my God." (Ruth 1:16 - NKJV).

Poverty, death, and social discrimination are some of the struggles on this road to success. But there is one thing for sure: God remains faithful to those who are loyal to him.

DAVID AND GOLIATH

David's story, particularly his battle with Goliath, illustrates resilience and faith in the face of hardship. Despite being a young shepherd underestimated by others, David faced numerous challenges, including rejection from his family and threats from King Saul.

His preparation involved years of protecting his flocks from predators, which instilled courage and skill in him.

Goliath, a giant warrior, challenged the Israelite army to send out the champion to fight him. David, a young shepherd, volunteered to fight despite his lack of experience in battle. Armed only with a sling and five smooth stones, he confronted Goliath, who was heavily armored and armed with a sword and spear. David, trusting in God's power, slung a stone that struck Goliath in his forehead, causing the giant to fall. David used the giant's sword to defeat him, winning the battle for Israel. This victory not only demonstrated David's courage and faith in God but also marked the beginning of his rise to prominence in Israel. His famous declaration emphasized trust over fear: "The battle is the Lord's" (see 1 Samuel 17:47, 2 Chronicles 20:15).

JEREMIAH, THE PROPHET

Jeremiah is known as the "weeping prophet." He faced many hardships throughout his life, including persecution, imprisonment, and personal loss. His triumphs can be attributed to several key factors. Jeremiah maintained a deep faith in God, which provided him with strength and purpose even in the face of adversity. His unwavering commitment to his prophetic mission helped him endure hardships.

Despite all the danger Jeremiah faced, he boldly conveyed God's messages, often warning of impending doom and calling for repentance. His willingness to confront powerful leaders and societal norms highlighted his bravery.

Jeremiah displayed remarkable resilience, continuing his work despite rejection and suffering. Even when it seemed futile, his ability to persevere in his mission highlighted his inner strength. Jeremiah found support in God's guidance throughout his struggles, which fortified him during challenging times. Jeremiah also conveyed messages of hope and restoration, particularly in his later prophecies. This vision allowed him to look beyond immediate troubles and maintain a sense of purpose.

Through these qualities, Jeremiah endured his hardships and fulfilled his role as a vital messenger of faith and hope for future generations. The prophet Jeremiah continued to preach and prophesy in the Lord's name. His story exemplifies what it means to praise God in challenging times.

Through the Lord's mercies, we are not consumed, because His compassions fail not. They are new every morning; Great is Your faithfulness. "The Lord is my portion," says my soul, "Therefore I hope in Him!" (Lamentations 3:22-24 - NKJV).

Like Jeremiah, we must not be afraid to persevere for the truth, even if the world persecutes us for our faith.

JOB, A GOOD MAN

Job was a wealthy, blameless man in the land of Oz. Why do dreadful things happen to good people? People use Job's story to answer this question.

God permits Satan to test Job's faith because Satan believed Job would only remain faithful in life when he was without struggles. Job received reports about the loss of his properties and children in one day. He developed terrible skin sores, and his wife insisted that Job denounce God. The course that Job's life took would suggest the absence of God. Yet, Job continued to praise God, and he trusted the process and proclaimed the praises of God.

And he said: "Naked I came from my mother's womb, and naked shall I return there. The Lord gave, and the Lord has taken away; Blessed be the name of the Lord." (Job 1:21 - NKJV).

The person closest to Job's heart was his wife; she urged him to blaspheme God and end his life, but Job remained steadfast in his belief in God.

"Why am I struggling?" should never be a question to ask God. Even if we lose everything, there is a reason for the struggles in our lives. In the end, struggles with faith can strengthen us. We should never entertain the thought of giving up on the journey, even when it seems dim and gray.

PETER, THE APOSTLE

Peter was known to be the leader of the twelve apostles, but his struggles as a follower of Christ were all prophecies documented in the Bible. He was remarkable to Jesus because he displayed deep faith in Jesus Christ, the Son of God (see Matthew 16:15-18 and Mark 8:29).

Peter, originally named Simon Peter, and his brother, Andrew, worked as fishermen when Jesus called them to join Him. Jesus also identified Peter as the 'rock' upon which He would build His church. Peter is known for denying Jesus three times after Jesus was arrested and for leading the early church after Jesus' death. He witnessed Jesus' miracles and became the apostles' leader despite his occasional doubt about Jesus.

The first miracle Peter witnessed was when Jesus cured his mother-in-law, who had a high fever. He saw the feeding of the five thousand. Jesus multiplied two fish and five loaves of bread to feed five thousand people. After the miracle of the loaves and fish, the gospel of Matthew, Mark, and John portrays Jesus walking on the water. The apostles were on a boat waiting for Jesus to return. After praying, the water became very rough, tossing it violently. The apostles saw someone walking on the water coming towards them. They became afraid, thinking they saw a ghost until Jesus called and identified Himself.

And Peter answered Him and said, "Lord, if it is You, command me to come to You on the water." (Matthew 14:28 - NKJV).

Jesus called Peter to Him, but as Peter stepped out into the water, he became afraid and began to sink. Jesus caught him and chastised him for his doubt and lack of faith in Him. Despite Peter's doubt, Jesus still singled him out as particularly important to His mission.

When Jesus came into the region of Caesarea Philippi, He asked His disciples, saying, "Who do men say that I, the Son of Man, am?" So, they said, "Some say John the Baptist, some Elijah, and others Jeremiah or one of the prophets." He said to them, "But who do you say that I am?" Simon Peter answered and said, "You are the Christ, the Son of the living God." Jesus answered and said to him, "Blessed are you, Simon Bar-Jonah, for flesh and blood has not revealed this to you, but My Father who is in heaven. And I also say to you that you are Peter, and on this rock, I will build My church, and the gates of Hell shall not prevail against it. And I will give you the keys of the kingdom of heaven, and whatever you bind on earth will be bound in heaven, and whatever you loose on earth will be loosed in heaven. (Matthew 16:13-19 – NKJV).

Peter was one of the first apostles. While he was a fisherman, he followed John the Baptist, which ultimately allowed Jesus to choose him as an early disciple or follower. When walking on water towards Jesus, he lost faith and sank. He denied knowing Jesus three times. After Jesus' resurrection, Peter persevered to overcome his spiritual and personal struggles to show that he genuinely believed in Jesus.

He said to him the third time, "Simon, son of Jonah, do you love Me?" Peter was grieved because He said to him the third time, "Do you love Me?" And he said to Him, "Lord, You know all things; You know that I love You." Jesus said to him, "Feed My sheep." (John 21:17 – NKJV).

This was a leap of faith displayed by Peter.

Despite our imperfections, Jesus still spent the time to redeem us to Himself. It does not matter how far we have wandered; Jesus always forgives us and brings us to victory.

THE BLEEDING WOMAN

The story of the bleeding woman found in Matthew, Mark, and Luke's gospels emphasizes the importance of suffering before achievement and triumph. According to this story, a woman who had experienced continuous bleeding for over twelve years came to Jesus with the hope of being healed. She thought she would be healed if she could touch the hem of His garment. She was able to touch Jesus' coat despite the throng around Him; her bleeding stopped immediately. The lady confessed when Jesus realized that virtue had left His body. He comforted her by saying, *"Daughter, your faith hath made you whole. Go in peace and be freed from your suffering." (James 5:34 - KJV).*

This story highlights the importance of faith and healing and the worth of not giving up but pressing through one's fears and adversities until one achieves the desired results. Her trust in God brought her a miracle.

MARY AND MARTHA

The story of Mary and Martha shows two different approaches to following Jesus (see Luke 10:38-42). Martha worked hard to welcome

Jesus to her home. Her sister, Mary of Bethany, just sat at the feet of Jesus and listened. Both Mary and Martha served, yet Mary understood the priority or the necessity of choosing to abide with Christ. Martha was distracted by her many tasks, so she came to Him asking him to tell Mary to help her. But Jesus replied, *"Martha, Martha, you are worried and troubled about many things. But one thing is needed, and Mary has chosen that good part, which will not be taken away from her. (Luke 10:41-42 – NKJV).*

Mary, the more contemplative sister, chose to sit at Jesus' feet and listen to His teachings when He visited their home, and Martha, overwhelmed with tasks, rebuked her. Jesus affirmed that Mary had chosen the better path (see Luke 10:38-42). Mary's trials were balancing her devotion to Jesus with the expectation of others, but her focus on His word brought her spiritual victory. Later, when their brother Lazarus died, Martha initially expressed sorrow and doubt, but Mary, though grieving, also showed unwavering faith in Jesus' power. Jesus raised Lazarus from the dead, demonstrating that their trials were met with God's glory and triumph over death (see John 11:1-44). Both sisters' journeys reflect how faith in Jesus, even amidst hardship, leads to divine triumph.

Let's examine the circumstances in the story just related. Martha demonstrated:

- **Defensiveness**: Martha defended her place, stating that her sister left her alone to serve.
- **Dismissiveness**: Martha depersonalizes Mary as "my sister" as though Mary was not even her sister.
- **Desperation**: Martha attempts to control the situation—and Jesus—with her comment about being "alone."
- **Disbelief:** Martha asks, "Do You not care?"

Martha's distracted serving led to a place she did not want to go. Martha regretted how she spoke to Jesus, but He lovingly acknowledged the state of her heart with a tender tone and repetition. Jesus invited her to consider a way of serving without distraction or self-righteousness. In Martha's mind, she had no choice but to serve alone with much worry, but Jesus reminded her that she did not have a choice. Jesus did not mind Mary sitting at His feet. He unequivocally applauded it; He praised it. Jesus affirmed Mary as His disciple as well as her choice to abide with Him. Jesus declares that one thing is needed as His disciple: to abide in Him.

Many of us desire to follow God's call by serving Him with everything we have, but we can easily find ourselves overcommitted. Being worried and troubled about many things is a distraction. We live in a culture that exalts 'multitasking' and 'we-can-do-it-all.' That is a wrong mentality to have. We need to adopt and learn God's priorities.

We have been given gifts to express God's love. In our appointed generation, we have a unique expression in the body of Christ, but if you are not trying to do it all, then you are driven to distraction. We must remain and abide in Jesus by humbly sitting at His feet. By doing that, we will absorb His love.

I am the vine; you are the branches. He who abides in Me, and I in him, bears much fruit; for without Me, you can do nothing. (John 15:5 - NKJV).

Many are like Martha, but we can learn from Mary. On this journey to success, distraction is sometimes described as "cumbered." There is enough to hinder, hamper, and obstruct us, but Christ desires us to be courageous and fight our way through with his help. No matter how it looks, all that is expected of us is to abide at the feet of Jesus. It is awesome to receive His invitation to sit at His feet.

What does it feel like to be covered by the weight of self-imposed responsibility, anxiety, and control? Jesus says:

"Come to Me, all you who labor and are heavy laden, and I will give you rest. Take My yoke upon you and learn from Me, for I am gentle and lowly in heart, and you will find rest for your souls. For My yoke is easy and My burden is light." (Matthew 11:28-30 - NKJV).

These words are so fitting. The one who sits at Jesus' feet learns that His yoke is easy and delightful. With Jesus' yoke, there is no work for us; Jesus invites us to lean on Him, and we will have a safe journey on this road to success. God will show you how to make this journey successful. Walk with God and depend on Him wholeheartedly.

Many can identify with Martha or Mary. So many get distracted and pull away from Jesus. What is the result? Trouble and life end up in disarray.

Sitting at Jesus' feet, as viewed by the culture and world around us, even by church people, seems weird. Some do not believe we can sit at Jesus' feet and learn from Him. The moral of this story with Martha and Mary is that we should not be distracted by tasks like Martha and miss being with Jesus like Mary. If we study these scriptures, we realize that Jesus spent much time with these two sisters, yet they believed in the future but wrestled with the "now."

Jesus is who He says He is. Jesus knew He had the power to raise Lazarus to life that same day. Our only responsibility is to trust God. That is all He asks us to do. We sadly continue to question God with the loss of a loved one and many other situations, some of which we label "unanswered prayers," but we must learn to accept what is done by God is well done. No matter how we feel about it, His divine will should also be our will.

Debrakay M. Brown

At the end of the day, It is all to God's glory.

Studying these biblical characters, we can see who suffered hardships but emerged successfully. This should strengthen our faith and trust in our God. Each individual encountered significant trials but overcame them through faith, perseverance, and sometimes divine intervention by God. God is our only source of survival as we journey on the road to success. Our desire should be more of Jesus daily. Trusting God is fundamental as we navigate life's journey for distinct reasons.

We need God's guidance and direction as we trust Him for a higher plan for our lives. He is willing and able to assist us in making decisions and facing our everyday challenges with confidence, knowing that we are part of a greater design.

If we are in this life, we should be prepared to face difficulties and adversities, but our trust in God offers comfort and strength, helping us to endure hardships with resilience and hope. Our trust in God acts as an anchor during turbulent times. Trusting in God's plan helps us find purpose in our experiences, struggles, and setbacks. It offers a perspective that our trials have meaning and contribute to our growth and the fulfillment of a divine plan.

Our faith in God inspires hope and optimism, even when situations seem bleak. This hope can be a powerful motivator, encouraging us to persevere and maintain a positive outlook. Trusting God in any situation connects us with a supportive community of believers. This shared faith provides encouragement, practical support, and a sense of belonging as we journey together. Trusting God provides a foundation of faith that supports, guides, and sustains us through life's ups and downs. It transforms our perspective, enabling us to navigate our path with greater assurance and peace.

After reading about these people of God who triumphed despite their struggles, here are some questions that would be beneficial for you to answer. These questions should help determine how these stories inspired you:

- How did the obstacles these men of God faced and the victories they won help you realize that all things are possible when you put your trust in God?
- How can adversities shape leadership and spiritual guidance?
- How do triumphs impact your community or your household?
- Can you identify any common traits or strategies among these people that you think contributed to their success?
- How can you maintain your faith and commitment during tough times?
- What lessons have you learned from the experiences of the men and women you read about that you can apply to your own life?
- How did their struggles influence their understanding of divine purpose or calling?
- How did their triumphs affect their relationship with others, including family, peers, and congregants?
- Are there any specific turning points in their stories that are particularly significant to you?

Chapter 7

The Triumph of Resilience

There are some famous men and women who also experienced obstacles on their road to success. We will discuss some of them.

ALBERT EINSTEIN

Albert Einstein had trouble speaking for the first three years of life. Despite this, he still received good grades throughout primary and elementary school. Einstein was always said to be very forgetful; he was forgetful throughout his entire life. Some people said he had dyslexia, but this was never proven. However, with all those speculations, he did so well that he was selected to attend the gymnasium in Germany.

In Germany, where Einstein grew up, there were three types of high schools. The gymnasium is the one that is academically focused and where the brightest students go. He would not have been chosen to go there if his work in his early years was not exemplary. He was extremely focused on Math and Physics. His teachers believed he was a lazy child because he was constantly distracted by abstract concepts. Many adults around expressed a lack of confidence in him, but he excelled above all the negativities and instead developed the theory of **"Relativity."**

Albert Einstein is often considered the most influential physicist of the 20th century. He is known for his many contributions to Science and Mathematics, including the "Theory of General Relativity." This theory explains gravity as a natural result of mass in space and predicts the existence of gravitational waves. This theory helps scientists understand how the universe works. He also developed the 'theory of light.' Einstein proposes that light is made up of particles called photons with properties of both waves and particles. This theory laid the foundation for quantum mechanics and has practical applications on television. He went on to introduce *"The explanation of the photoelectric effect."* Published in 1905, this was the first experimental proof of energy quantization. Einstein hypothesizes that light is not emitted or absorbed continuously but rather in discrete packages of energy, which he called "quanta" (later named quantum). He explained that the energy (E) of these quanta is proportional to the frequency(f) of the light with the relationship: ($E=hf$)

Einstein, who had problems speaking in his earlier years, made a notable contribution to Mathematics, which led Einstein to encourage Mathematicians to develop multidimensional geometries. According to his teachers, this same "lazy boy" was credited with inventing several other things, including the "Einstein refrigerator," gas absorption heat pump, sound reproduction apparatus, and self-adjusting cameras based on light intensity.

This hypothesis was a key development in understanding energy quantization and played a crucial role in the early development of quantum theory. Einstein's work provides the theoretical basis for the electric effect, showing that light will behave as discrete packets of energy, providing experimental support for energy quantization. This discovery eventually contributed to the development of quantum mechanics.

His theories of relativity led to important advances, including coding the inside of a refrigerator, guess observation, heat pumps, solar production apparatus, and self-adjusting cameras based on light. His theories of relativity led to new ways of looking at time, space, matter, energy, and gravity. He was not an inventor, but his work led to many important advances. Albert Einstein's name is synonymous with a genius. He is one of the estuaries' greatest thinkers. Einstein made his name as a Physicist and Mathematician. His work later made important advances, including the control of atomic energy, space exploration, and the applications of light. He was just a simple young boy born to Jewish parents in Germany.

When he reached the age of fifteen years, one teacher remarked that there was nothing left to teach him. He studied at the Institute of Technology in Zurich and received his doctorate in 1905 at the age of twenty-six. He published five groundbreaking scientific papers that same year. The first paper earned him his doctorate, and the concepts presented in the next four papers helped change the understanding of the universe. The topics were:

- **Brownian movement** or the zigzag motions of microscopic particles in suspension. Einstein's findings helped prove the existence of atoms and molecules.
- **The quantum theory of light.** Einstein proposed that light is composed of separate packets of energy called **Quanta and photons;** they have the same properties as particles and some properties of waves. He also explained the **photoelectric effect**, which is the emission of electrons from some solids when they are struck by light. Television is a practical application of Einstein's theory of light.
- **The special theory of relativity.** Einstein explained that time and motion are relative to their observers—as long as the speed

of light remains constant and natural laws are the same throughout the universe.
- **The link between mass and energy.** The fourth paper expanded on this idea with the famous equation $E=mc2$, relating mass and energy. This formula demonstrates that a small particle of matter contains enormous energy. This forms much of the basis for nuclear energy.

After Einstein presented a series of groundbreaking ideas in 1905, he continued to research and expand these concepts and other ideas in Physics and Mathematics. In 1916, Einstein presented the general theory of relativity, proposing that gravity is a curved field in the space-time continuum created by the existence of mass.

In 1921, he received the Nobel Prize in Physics for his discovery of the law of the photoelectric effect and his work in theoretical physics. Einstein eventually left his homeland in Germany in 1933 upon Adolf Hitler's rise to power and accepted a position at the Institute of Advanced Study in Princeton, NJ. He became a U.S. citizen in 1940. He was peaceful by nature, and he spoke out strongly against nationalism, war, and violence. He also supported Zionism—the idea of the creation of a homeland for Jews in Palestine.

In 1939, Einstein learned that two German chemists had split the uranium atom; he wrote to the then-US president, Franklin D. Roosevelt, that this application of scientific knowledge could lead to Germany's development of an atomic bomb, and he urged the United States to begin its research. His suggestion led to the creation of the Manhattan Project and the first two atomic bombs it spawned. In 1945, Einstein was saddened when he heard of the destruction caused by the two nuclear bombs dropped on Japan and later campaigned for a brand of nuclear weapon.

Scientists are still finding new uses for Einstein's work today. He developed a refrigerator design that received a US patent in 1930. Instead of cooling the interior of the refrigerator as we know it today, Einstein's design uses ammonia butane water and almost no energy. Researchers are taking another look at the design as an eco-friendly alternative to air conditioning and refrigeration.

Einstein helped the world. His theories led to new ways of looking at time, space, matter, energy, and gravity. This was the same guy his teacher believed was lazy and would not come out with anything good.

Tony Robbins said in a quote, *"It is in your moment of decision that your destiny is shaped."*

Catherine Pulsifer said, *"Life presents many choices; the choices we make determine our future."*

Koifman said, *"Control your destiny or someone else will."*

Pinterest said, *"Never let anyone decide your future; never allow your circumstances to define your destiny."*

Epictetus said, *"It's not what happens to you, but how you react to it that matters."*

I believe that a brilliant way to have a destiny is simply to choose one. Whatever you make up in your mind to become, that will be the person you will be. If you continue living, not changing directions, you may end up where you plan to be.

Anthon St. Maarten.com states, *"You cannot wait for others to decide your fate, you can master your destiny. Just know that others* seldom have very much planned for your future happiness, so the do-it-yourself approach may be your best bet."

Albert Ellis states, *"The best years of your life are the ones in which you decide your problems on your own, you do not blame them on anyone or anything. You'll realize that you control your destiny."*

Never allow negative people to speak into your life or try to discourage you on your journey. You can succeed if you want to succeed; it doesn't matter who doesn't believe in you as long as you believe in yourself.

Let us look at another person who had difficulties on the road to success. However, despite the difficulties, he came out successful.

VINCENT VAN GOGH

Gogh was a Dutch post-impressionist painter. He was known for his unique technique, which included bold colors and sweeping brush strokes. His work is also known for its contoured forms and emphatic brushwork. This man sold only one painting during his life. It was sold for 400 francs in Belgium, seven months before his death. He produced over 900 paintings, yet only the "Red Vineyard" was sold while he was alive. He might not have physically overcome his challenges, but his dedication and persistence in his work, despite receiving no monetary compensation or external praise, is still something to be commended.

Despite Vincent's setbacks, he is considered one of the most famous and influential figures in Western art history. In just over a decade, he created around 2,100 artworks, including 860 oil paintings. Vincent struggled with poverty. After Vincent's death, his brother wanted nothing more than to raise the profile of his brother's work. Six months later, he passed away. His widow, Jo Van Gogh-Bonger, set about completing the task. She sold some of Vincent's work, loaned others out for exhibitions, and, very importantly, published his letters to Theo. Van Gogh's fascinating life story is one of the reasons why his work took the whole world by storm.

One of his painting portraits of Dr. Gachet was sold for 148.6 million in 1990. Although he did not become famous before he died, his commitment to excel was his aim. He became known as the most famous painter that ever existed.

There is no need to give up if your dreams are not realized. Commend yourself for what you have achieved. Just be your greatest fan and encourage yourself.

Let us look together at another person who experienced hardships on his road to success.

JIM CARREY

Jim Carrey is a Canadian-born and also a U.S. citizen since 2004. He is an actor and producer famous for his rubbery body movements and flexible facial expressions. At fifteen years old, Jim Carrey dropped out of school to support his family. Soon after, he and his family had no other choice but to live in a van. These were challenging times for him on his journey to success. Despite this, Carrey continued to follow his dream of becoming a comedian. He is a two-time Golden Globe winner.

Jim rose from childhood homelessness to becoming a famous actor. He is famous for his movie roles, including "How the Grinch Stole Christmas." Many people don't know that Carrey's childhood wasn't always filled with jokes and laughs. He experienced tremendous challenges. As a teenager, he began doing stand-up comedy and started down a path that would culminate in fame and success.

Carrey was the youngest of four children. His mother, Kathleen, worked as a stay-at-home mom, and his father, Percy, was a saxophone player and an accountant. Life was not easy for young Carrey. His mother suffered from chronic health issues, and his father struggled to support his family. Carrey would spend hours in his room making funny faces in front of a mirror to cope with all this stress. So, he developed a talent for impressions, which would later make him famous. He was incredibly determined to succeed as a comedian at an incredibly early age. When he was ten, he sent his resume to the producer of the Carol Burton Show.

This was an exceedingly difficult time in his life, which made him very angry. Fortunately, he chose to focus on humor instead of anger. Carrey's comedic talents turned things around for him. He got his first big break in comedy after his family experienced homelessness. He landed a stand-up gig at Yuk Yuk's Comedy Club in Toronto. In 2017, People Magazine interviewed him. He said he went for a tryout and he was booed off the stage. But that less-than-stellar first appearance did not stop Carrey. He continued to perform, and by 1979, he was earning a living with his acts. What happened next was interesting. Carrey was performing as the opening act for famous comedians, including Rodney Dangerfield. He became known for his high energy and a repertoire of impressions. The rest, as they say, is history. Despite all the setbacks in his earlier years, he pushed forward and became a victor on this same road to success which is paved with hardships.

Here goes another person whose trial ended in triumph.

THOMAS EDISON

Thomas Edison was an American inventor and businessperson. He played a significant role in introducing the modern age of electricity. His inventions include electricity, utility systems, the light bulb, recorded sound, motion pictures, R&D labs, and the alkaline family of storage batteries. Edison is best known for the invention of the light bulb. He is also known for the improvement of the telegraph and telephone system. Thomas Edison's famous quote was, *"I have not failed; I have just found 10,000 ways that won't work."*

As a child, Thomas Edison experienced scarlet fever and ear infections—deafness and a blow to the head left him with hearing difficulties in both ears. By age twelve, he was deaf in one ear and nearly deaf in the other. Some people say that his deafness motivated his inventions. He was overly optimistic and good-natured and would not quit.

When you have tried and failed, try again. You will finally achieve success if you do not give up. Success came for Edison by mastering his defeats. Success lies not in achieving what you aim for but in aiming at what you ought to achieve. Do not worry about doubters or the opposition around you. **Doctor Bob Jones** says in one of his quotes, *"The door to the room of success swings on hinges of opposition."* No rule of success will ever work if you do not remember that success comes from mastering defeat.

STEPHEN EDWIN KING

Stephen King, an American author, drafted novels, short stories, and non-fiction books. He is known as the "king of horror," but he also wrote in other genres, including suspense, crime, science fiction, fantasy, and mystery. King has written around two hundred short stories, most of which have been published in collections. King's story is significant and interesting. Thirty different publishers rejected him when he wrote his first novel. This made him upset, so he threw the novel in the trash.

His wife took it out and encouraged him to complete it. King's books have now sold over 350 million copies. The horror novel, Carrie, was written by King in 1974. It is a classic novel with many films and TV adaptations to its name. When you look at King's ordeal, it shows that setbacks did come on his road to success. Often, people just need a little bit of encouragement to overcome obstacles in their lives.

Trying times are not the time to quit trying. Too many people have this "finishing fever." Success may be near when it seems far away, so just stick to your fight. When you are hardest hit, when things seem the worst, that is when you should not quit. Remember, every cloud has a silver lining.

BENJAMIN FRANKLIN

Benjamin Franklin was a printer, inventor, scientist, and statesman. He was the 10th son of seventeen children for a man named Josiah Franklin, who made soap and candles. This was one of the lowest of the artisan crafts. He had one year in grammar school and another under a private teacher in his earlier years. Their formal education ended at age ten. At age twelve, he was apprenticed to his brother James, who was a printer. Benjamin read tirelessly and taught himself to write effectively. He loved poetry but was discouraged by its quality, so he gave it up.

He read several papers repeatedly. He copied and recopied them, then tried to recall them from memory. He even turned those readings into poetry and then back into prose. As all the founders did, Franklin realized that writing comes competently and was such a rare talent in the eighteenth century that anyone who could do it well drew attraction. Prose writing became particularly important, and this became of really good use to him during his life. In 1721, Franklin founded a weekly newspaper called the News England Courant, the first newspaper in Boston. Readers were invited to contribute to the paper. Benjamin was just a simple apprentice, so Ben started writing letters at night and signing them with the name of a fake fictional widow, Silence Dogwood. Dogwood had so much advice and was so critical of the world around her, especially how women were treated. Ben would sneak the letters under the door at night. This way, no one would know who was writing the pieces. He sent fourteen letters in all.

He intended to present letters once monthly with a short epistle, which he believed would add meaning to the reader's entertainment. These letters were published in the New England Courant fortnightly and amused readers. Eventually, James found out these writings were done by his younger brother, and this made him furious. Benjamin ended his apprenticeship without permission and fled to Philadelphia, then to London, and then back to Philadelphia, where he set up a print shop and began to publish in The Pennsylvania Gazette. The writing was exceptionally good; everyone wanted to know who was responsible for these writings. He occupies a very outstanding place in U.S. history. He did not only play a significant role in the Revolutionary War Era and the fight for America and independence, but he also helped to shape the US Constitution and vision for the new nation.

Ben encountered financial setbacks that could not stop him from going after an education. He conquered this by reading intensely and used that to help educate himself. His brother was mad and amazed when he found out Ben was doing well. He ran away just to avoid conflict with his brother, but that did not stop him. He journeyed this rough, rocky, uncertain road to success. What a blessing to keep chasing your dreams. This is when you become unstoppable.

Winston Churchill said, *"Success is not final; failure is not fatal. It is the courage to continue that counts."*

Debrakay M. Brown

BETHANY HAMILTON

Bethany Hamilton is an American professional surfer and writer. In 2003, Bethany survived a horrific accident where a shark bit off her left arm while surfing. She was only thirteen years old. Instead of admitting defeat, one month later, she went right back to her surfing board and continued to practice. Two years later, she won first place in the Explorer Women's Division of the NSSA National Championship.

She served as a real inspiration to people when she returned to surfing. She has a heroic ability, and that helped to provide people with hope. She provided hope for countless individuals. This is what you call overcoming a difficult obstacle. Giving up is not welcome on this road to success.

WALT DISNEY

Walt Disney was an American animator, film producer, voice actor, and entrepreneur. He was famous as an animator for cartoon films and a creator of cartoon characters like Mickey Mouse and Donald Duck. Disney has always wanted to influence people's lives. Walt never wanted to be boring or just to be known as a man who did not have a childhood because his father always pushed him around. He desperately wanted to be a success in life, and he wanted the name Walt Disney to be remembered, and for sure, it will be remembered.

He was employed at the Kansas City Star. This was his first job. His newspaper editor fired him and told him he lacked creativity and imagination. He drove to Disney's animation studio Laugh-O-gram a few years later.

He moved to California to produce cartoons, and his career took off. He made it from the pages of a book to the television screen. He created a family-oriented theme park that was based on popular beloved cartoon characters and imaginations, from Cinderella's Castle to the famous Main Street, USA. There is something extraordinary lying around every corner. Walt Disney World, otherwise known as the happiest place on Earth or the place where dreams come true, was founded by a man who dreamed of creating a place where children and parents could spend time together while making amazing memories. This amazing park is only one of Walt Disney's greatest achievements. Right after his early setbacks, he made it.

These inspiring people may seem unreal at times, but their stories are so telling. We can learn from them; they did not give up on their journey. They overcame adversities; yes, they were real people who experienced challenges, but they never allowed the challenges to prevent them from making their lives successful.

The situations we face in life can be incredibly challenging, but we need to rest on the promises of God. God promised us protection during our rough and dark days. He will still be there while you are on the bumpy, rough, winding road to success. **Psalm 32:7** states: *"You are a hiding place for me; you preserve me from trouble. You surround me with shouts of deliverance. I will instruct you and teach you the way you should go. I will counsel you with my eyes upon you." (AMP).*

Psalm 34:7 says, *"Right now, the angel of the Lord encamps around those who fear him and delivers them." (NIV).* God commands his angels to protect those who seek his protection **(see Psalm 91:11).**

Psalm 46:1-3 says, *"God is our refuge and strength, a very present help in trouble. Therefore, we will not fear, even though the earth be removed, and though the mountains be carried into the midst of the sea; Though its waters roar and be troubled, though the mountains shake with its swelling. Selah." (NKJV).*

Psalm 91:1 says, *"He who dwells in the secret place of the Most High shall abide under the shadow of the Almighty." (NKJV).*

This demonstrates complete faith and confidence in God as a protector who will keep people safe and inspire them to seek refuge in Him and grow in His shadow.

Psalm 91:9-14 says, *"Because you have made the Lord, who is my refuge, even the Most High, your dwelling place, no evil shall befall you, nor shall any plague come near your dwelling; For He shall give His angels charge over you, to keep you in all your ways. In their hand*s, *they shall bear you up, lest you dash your foot against a stone. You shall tread upon the lion and the cobra, the young lion and the serpent you shall trample underfoot. "Because he has set his love upon Me, therefore I will deliver him; I will set him on high because he has known my name." (NKJV).*

No matter how old or young you are, the word of God is there to sustain you. It is always relevant irrespective of age, color, or nationality.

Isaiah 46:4 states, *"Even to your old age, I am He, and even to gray hairs I will carry you! I have made, and I will bear; even I will carry, and will deliver you." (NKJV).*

Our confidence in God, our never-failing friend and defender, should be unstoppable. He is a promise-keeper, our good shepherd, mighty God, alpha and omega, beginning and the end. We should keep our confidence in God, no matter what we face.

Mark 11:24 states, *"Therefore I say to you, whatever things you ask when you pray, believe that you receive them, and you will have them." (NKJV).* How difficult does your journey seem at times? When things seem like they are getting out of hand, it is the best time to throw yourself carelessly in your Master's hand. God told us in **1 Corinthians 10:13,** *"No temptation has overtaken you except such as is common to man; but God is faithful, who will not allow you to be tempted beyond what you are able, but with the temptation will also make the way of escape, that you may be able to bear it." (NKJV).* God is faithful and will never let temptation take us out or go beyond what He knows. He can bear us in His arms. He further promised to make a way to escape. He will make all things possible so we can endure. We can find strength in God's Word during uncertain times.

Do not forget that we will encounter demanding situations and different seasons while we pursue this journey, but even in our darkest moments, His promises remain unchanged and unshaken. He told us He would help us no matter what. **Psalm 34:18** reminds us that He is near those who have a broken heart. He promises to always stay with us. When our spirits seem crushed, God draws closer to us. When our spirits are broken, He engulfs us with His arms of protection. It is important to know or remember that He has already told us that He is our refuge and strength, a present help in times of trouble.

When we are hurting, we have a consolation. He will administer help to our weary souls. It is okay to feel that He is far away, but remember that He would never allow His child to experience a certain difficulty without His permission. Absolutely nothing happens to us without his permission, as long we are abiding by His will.

Romans 8:28 says, *"And we know that all things work together for good to those who love God, to those who are the called according to His purpose." (NKJV).*

These words are so encouraging. We need to trust God wholeheartedly. His plan for our lives is tailored specifically for us.

The situations and circumstances may seem hard and even unbearable, but God will still bring the good out of the worst circumstances. We need to learn to trust the process and continue our journey without worrying about what people may say or think about us.

Be reminded that you are not what people think or say. You are much more than people's thoughts or opinions. You are wonderfully and fearfully made, and there is no limit to your success. Take the limits off God and watch Him work mightily on your behalf.

While on this journey, you cannot afford to be weak and cranky, crying, whining, and complaining about everything. Listen carefully; you serve a great, big, wonderful God; therefore, no matter what, you should always have praise on your lips. Jump, leap, skip for joy if you need to. Never be afraid to praise your deliverer because He inhabits our praise. Never allow your past failures to dictate the outcome of your present situation. Your past failures should not prevent you from walking into your bright future.

God promised to pour out His blessing upon us from the windows of heaven. All we need to do is be faithful, hold our side of the bargain, and watch God work. We are heirs to His throne, and the enemy, that deceiver of our souls, is very much aware of the greatness inside of us, so he produces his tricks and hellish schisms and plans to destroy us and throw us off track.

As you journey, remember the enemy desires to crush you, preventing you from ending your journey successfully. The speed bumps, potholes, and large puddles are very evident; some can also be at hidden spots. The winding roads and narrow bridges are also there to turn you off course, aiming at hindering your progress. Speed bumps are there too, but these can serve to alert other pilgrims to exercise spiritual intelligence so they can see things as they are and not just what they want them to be. There are incredibly wise ways to respond to these speed bumps on your journey. Some of these ways are to listen for that still small voice of your Savior, start rejoicing, examine the truth of the circumstance you are facing, confess your sins, slow down, stop, look, listen, turn from sin, develop and restore that friendship and communication with God.

These questions that follow can facilitate deeper understanding and discussion about resilience, hard work, and success in the face of adversity:

- Which individual's story of overcoming hardship resonates with you most and why?
- What key factors or sources of strength helped these individuals endure their struggles?
- How did hardships shape their character and contribute to their eventual success?
- What role did family, friends, or mentors play in their journey through adversity?
- What specific lessons about resilience can we learn from their experiences?
- What pivotal moments or decisions contributed to their breakthrough in overcoming hardship?
- How did their success influence or inspire others facing similar challenges?
- How did these individuals handle feelings of doubt or fear during difficult times?
- How did their experience of hardship shape their future goals or aspirations?
- What strategies or mindset can we adopt from their stories to better cope with our challenges?

NOTES

Chapter 8

Different Seasons on the Journey to Success

You will experience different seasons as you journey on this road to success. Never allow the word "success" to be mistaken for all joy and grandeur; neither should it scare you when different challenges appear. Some of these seasons you will encounter are similar to the natural seasons we experience from day to day. These are winter, summer, spring, or fall. The spiritual seasons of life mirror the seasons of nature. People go through different seasons at contrasting times. Some people might have a season of winter, while others might have their season of spring simultaneously. It should be noted that every individual experiences their seasons at different periods of their life.

SPIRITUAL WINTER

This is a time of rest where a person can seize the opportunity to search for oneself, recharge, and hear the voice of God. It can also be a fun time for conversion, preparation by fasting and prayer, and waiting for answers. It is a great time to find delight in meditating. It can be a time when God does His work behind the scenes. On the other hand, during this time, you may feel cold in spirit, lack energy, and even refuse to do the things that normally bring you joy.

SPIRITUAL FALL

During this time, things can fall away. This can be a suitable time to grow, trust, and build your confidence in God. This time can be an appropriate time to reflect on things that might be holding you back. This can also be a time of releasing things that burden us, making it a time of transformation.

SPIRITUAL SPRING

This can be the early stage of planting ideas and seeing things blossom. Spring can be a spiritual metaphor for renewal or rebirth through Christ. During this time, Christians can plant ideas that come to them during winter and watch them begin to blossom. It is a time for spiritual refreshment.

SPIRITUAL SUMMER

This is the warmest season with the longest days. It is a time for growth, renewal, rest, and communion with God. There should be real signs of growth and blossoming; it is a wonderful time to harvest souls. Because of the hot days, grass and plants seem to dry up in the natural world, but trees that inhabit the grassland remain green and full of life. In the spiritual aspect of summer, this is a time when you can prove what you are made of and how firm you are planted; you can be put to the test. Summertime in nature is usually a time for rest and recreation, and so should it be in the spiritual aspect; it should be a time of connecting with God by basking in the sunshine of His love.

Some summer days might even be confused with winter and spring seasons; however, there are qualitative differences in the landscape of the soul in this season. We should crave to develop a deeper intimacy with God. The strength of our roots should be evaluated and proven. We should strive for the Holy Spirit to dwell deeply within us. Our intimacy with God should be and remain at its peak. We can safely say that, as believers, we should strive to maintain a good summer season throughout our spiritual journey.

Challenging times will be experienced in every season of our lives, but despite it all, God loves and cares for us, and we should strive to be brought into the beauty of His love. God uses seasons in our lives to allow us to grow and experience His care for us. Irrespective of the season we are in, He is still working His purpose out in our lives. We can relate to the seasons being called by different names as well.

Let us explore some of these seasons in more detail.

- The dry season.
- The grinding season.
- The test and trial season.
- The pruning season.
- The spiritual warfare season.
- The waiting season.

If you examine your current life, what season would you say you are in right now? Are you in the dry season waiting for something to happen? Or are you in the grinding season, where you are beaten up and purged? This season usually leads to the test and trial season. During this season, **1 Peter 1:7** states, *"that the genuineness of your faith, being much more precious than gold that perishes, though it is tested by fire, may be found to praise, honor, and glory at the revelation of Jesus Christ," (NKJV).*

Psalm 26:2 states, *"Examine me, O Lord, and prove me; Try my mind and my heart." (NKJV).*

Exodus 16:4 states, *"Then the Lord said to Moses, "Behold, I will rain bread from heaven for you. And the people shall go out and gather* *a certain quota every day, that I may test them, whether they will walk in My law or not." (NKJV).*

Jeremiah 17:10 states, *"I, the Lord, search the heart, I test the mind, even to give every man according to his ways, according to the fruit of his doings." (NKJV).*

ARE YOU IN SPIRITUAL WARFARE SEASON?

These are times when you are attacked by principalities, powers, and spiritual wickedness in high places. These attacks come anytime, sometimes during moving from one place to another, getting married, having children, studying, or trying to acquire a new home or a new job. Whatever you are doing at this time, it is the period where the advice is to be prepared for battle. Gird your heavenly armor on; wear it night and day. Ambush the lies of the evil one; watch and pray. We must be ready for spiritual warfare at any given time on this road to success.

There are some practices and weapons that Christians may use during spiritual warfare:

- **Prayer**
  We must pray at the beginning of every day, throughout the day, and before we go to bed. We need to be in constant prayer, as this is a crucial weapon of mass destruction.
- **Discerning**
  It is important to discern the difference between spiritual things and non-spiritual things.
- **Spirit of Peace**
  Rick Renner says that when peace operates in a person's life, they can walk through difficult places and situations without feeling it.

- **Truth**
  The scripture tells us to gird our loins with truth (see Ephesians 6:14). The first thing we should have is an understanding of the truth of the gospel. Remember, the devil is a master of lies and falsehood. He has everything designed to deceive the children of God, so if he can make God's children believe a lie rather than the truth, then he can get beneath our defenses and create havoc, causing all manners of destruction. We must trust Jesus, dismiss all doubts, and hold on to freedom and the truth. Victory must be ours.
- **Faith**
  We cannot emphasize too much how important this weapon of faith is. Faith is referred to as a shield, so when attacks come, you stand behind the shield of faith. The shield of faith will stop or extinguish all the flaming darts the devil attacks us with.
- **The Helmet of Salvation**
  This is designed to protect the head of a temporal soldier so the knowledge of salvation in Jesus Christ protects us. We should hold fast to the knowledge we have in Jesus Christ, and the process of salvation will always be alive and work within us.
- **The Sword of The Spirit**
  This is the Word of God that He has given us. We should try to learn and understand it. When we are immersed in the Word of God, we will have it at our disposal when attacked.

Other spiritual practices may include laying hands and anointing of oil, fasting with prayer, praise and worship.

We should ensure that we put on the whole armor of God and take a stand against the devil's schemes. Although we live in the world, we do not raise a war as the world does; we do not fight with literal weapons, which are weapons of the world. Spiritual weapons are powerful. They have divine power to demolish every stronghold, every contrary argument, whatever it is, all the bad setups that we may encounter.

Spiritual warfare can be easily detected; however, we cannot call everything spiritual warfare. All hardships in life should not be labeled as spiritual. As it is rightly said, do not look for a demon under every rock.

Sometimes the way we look at happenings and perceive them as spiritual warfare may be God evaluating and refining us, or it could just be us reaping what we have sown (see Psalm 66:10, 1 Peter 1:7, Proverbs 17:3, Galatians 6:7-8, and Proverbs 19:3).

We need to recognize the spiritual warfare seasons. Spiritual warfare often happens right before or after God uses us in a powerful ministry impact or before or after God moves in our lives in a mighty way. We must maintain our strength in the Lord and exercise our strength in God so we can manage during the different seasons of our lives. The change of seasons is unavoidable.

To everything, there is a season, a time for every purpose under heaven: (Ecclesiastes 3:1 - NKJV).

He has made everything beautiful in its time. Also, He has put eternity in their hearts, except that no one can find out the work that God does from beginning to end. (Ecclesiastes 3:11 - NKJV).

Being prepared for the changes means acknowledging the changes so there are no surprises.

THE DRY SEASON

This season is the time when God seems quiet, and sometimes you cannot even hear His voice or recognize His presence as you once did. God sometimes seems very distant. I can personally attest to some dry seasons in my personal life. It can be difficult at times. We feel empty, inadequate, dry, and situations seem hopeless. This is a very jarring experience when your life experiences do not line up with what you know to be true about God. You sometimes ask the question, "Where is God? God guides His children, so why can't I see Him? If God cares, why am I not seeing it or feeling it?"

The main key to mastering and challenging these rough seasons is acknowledging that you are in the season. Admit the season you are in, then draw closer to God, even when you feel He is far away. Keep pressing your way; keep focused on your goal; continue praying and reading the Word of God daily; talk to Him as your friend. When you experience great drought and dryness in a season, you tend to feel lonely and rejected, but remember **1 John 1:9**, *"If we confess our sins, He is faithful and just to forgive us our sins and to cleanse us from all unrighteousness." (NKJV).*

THE WAITING SEASON.

Psalm 37:7 says, *"Be still in the Lord and wait patiently for him; do not fret yourself over the one who prospers in his way or over the man who carries out evil devices."*

On this journey of life, you may be waiting for different things to change and for distinct reasons. It could be a change of job, a provision of a godly husband, waiting to be blessed with a biological child, or waiting for a place to call your home. Be encouraged; God will fulfill His promises in due time.

The season sometimes changes drastically from mildly annoying to maddening, from gravely discouraging to glorious victories. God often takes us through the tough seasons to land us to our best.

THE PRUNING SEASON

During this season, God chisels away the unwanted stuff. He takes or carves them away and prepares us for our next season. It does not matter how long the process takes; it is for His glory.

God wants to teach us how to wait. God knows exactly when and how to bring our waiting to an end. He is not going to rush or slow down the waiting but rather work His purpose out while we are waiting. God blesses us with different gifts; if we can recall, these gifts are usually given or refined while we wait. David cried out to the Lord in **Psalm 5:3,** *"My voice You shall hear in the morning, O Lord; in the morning I will direct it to You, and I will look up." (NKJV).*

God is listening and knows exactly where you are. God will not forget you.

THE GRINDING SEASON

This is a time when many of us find ourselves uncomfortable and uncertain. How many times do you say this, or do you hear this: "I don't have enough time to get everything done" or "Ah! I cannot be bothered; it's taking too long" or "No! No! I'm not ready yet!"

We sometimes find ourselves taken up with big projects, and at times, we do not even remember little people who require just a little bit of our time. Businesses have great value in our modern American culture, but as children of the highest, we should not crave, chase, or yearn after such while we leave our Savior out and even despise the poor and lowly. If we should find ourselves in the busy season of our lives, try to use up the time by chasing after God. The moment you realize you are blessed to see the dawning of a new day each morning, start using your time to give thanks and seek His direction immediately before you get too busy and automatically leave Him out of your daily diary. Recognize and plan what you need to get done each morning. Try to place your activities in the right order, then plow through those priorities accordingly. When you do this, it will help to alleviate your stress. It is important to give God His time as this will equip us adequately **(see John 15:5)**. Always rely on the Holy Spirit to lead and help you.

THE TEST AND TRIAL SEASON

One important thing you need to remember is that God is with you during all the trying times. When you are going through some hard times in your season, you might not understand what or why you are having that experience, but I am encouraging you that God sees and knows in due season. He will reveal to you the purpose of your circumstances as you journey.

"And let us not grow weary while doing good, for in due season we shall reap if we do not lose heart." (Galatians 6:9 – NKJV).

Fix your eyes on Jesus. Remember, there is no harm in keeping your mind focused on Jesus. The scripture states in **Colossians 3:2**, *"Set your mind on things above, not on things on the earth." (NKJV).* The temporary things of earth will perish, but the things of God are eternal. God understands every temptation we undergo. He also understands our pain, suffering, weaknesses, and shortcomings (see **Hebrews 4:15).**

"You have kept count of my tossing, my tears in your bottle, are they not in your book?" (Psalm 56:8 – NKJV).

Jesus knows just how it feels to be feeling sad (see **John 11:35**). He works through sadness to draw us to Himself, rouse us with a megaphone, and convict us of our desperate need for Him. (see **Matthew 7:13-14**).

When we are downtrodden, weary, and crushed beneath the suffering of this world, He is gentle and lowly and offers a light burden for our souls. *"Come to me, all you who are weary and burdened, and I will give you rest. Take my yoke upon you and learn from me, for I am gentle and humble in heart, and you will find rest for your souls. For my yoke is easy and my burden is light." (Matthew 11:28-30 - NIV).*

THE SPIRITUAL WARFARE SEASON

As you journey on this road paved with hardship, you must have a strong mind and profoundly serious determination. We must do as the writer says in **Ephesians 6:11-16,** *"Put on the whole armor of God, that you may be able to stand against the wiles of the devil. For we do not wrestle against flesh and blood, but against principalities, against powers, against the rulers of the darkness of this age, against spiritual hosts of wickedness in the heavenly places. Therefore, take up the whole armor of God, that you may be able to withstand in the evil day, and having done all, to stand. Stand therefore, having girded your waist with truth, having put on the breastplate of righteousness, and having shod your feet with the preparation of the gospel of peace; above all, taking the shield of faith with which you will be able to quench all the fiery darts of the wicked one." (NKJV).* We cannot afford to lose our grip on God while on this road. This is the only way to set ourselves up for failure. This journey to success is paved with hardships; however, keep your eyes on your goal.

Ecclesiastes. 9:11 states, *"I returned and saw under the sun that—The race is not to the swift, Nor the battle to the strong, Nor bread to the wise, Nor riches to men of understanding, Nor favor to men of skill, But time and chance happen to them all." (NKJV).*

Do not allow anyone you meet on this road to success who is getting ahead of you to let you feel you can't or you are not making it fast enough. Their strides might be longer than yours, but that is okay. Keep focused on your goal and your God-given potential, and fulfill your dreams. Failures will come at times, but they only serve to reveal the many miracles and victories won. These victories leave with us a testimony of winning. The doubters will be astonished to see how well you survived the battles and come out untouched. Remember, Daniel went through the lion's den and came out unhurt. Do not make rash or immature decisions when you are faced with challenging situations. During these moments, make your prayer for your daily needs.

Your heavenly Father knows what you need before you ask Him, but in everything, by prayer and supplication with thanksgiving, let your request be known to God (see **Matthew 6:8**). Do not accept failures. Use each challenge to propel you to another level.

Fear can cripple you—both in mind and spirit—and then, eventually, your entire being suffers. Fear is only a way the mind uses to tell you something is impossible. Never allow fear to stand in your way and cripple your success. Risks and dangers are real, so do not be fooled. Fear is a choice, but it is a bad one.

EMOTIONAL AND MENTAL DISTRESS

Mental and emotional strengths are of paramount importance and are often overlooked. You must be willing to examine your style of living. Try to identify the gray areas you need to work on. Unnecessary baggage is not permitted on this journey. The Word of God tells us in **Hebrews 12:1,** *"Therefore we also, since we are surrounded by so great a cloud of witnesses, let us lay aside every weight, and the sin which so easily ensnares us, and let us run with endurance the race that is set before us." (NKJV).*

The word "weight" in this verse comes from the Greek word "oikos" which means "burden." This is used to describe something so heavy that it prevents a runner from racing.

In the athletic field, the word describes when an athlete intentionally removes excess weight before a competition. In Hebrews 12:1, "weight" refers to *"incorrect actions and attitudes that can get in the way of running the spiritual race that is set before us."* This verse suggests that Christians should move these things from their lives and instead focus on Jesus, who began their faith and suffered on the cross. While traveling on the road to success, notice the warning signs strategically positioned for you to observe. We all know that as we drive on the temporal highways, we are given directions and instructions that we are expected to follow. The signs placed along the way include warnings of all kinds: speed limits, curves ahead, icy roads, construction work in progress, and many others. We know that we must be cautious on this road; otherwise, we could end up in great danger. Jesus ended His challenging sermon on the mount with a few warnings (see **Matthew 7:13-23).**

Enter in the straight gate, for wide is the gate, and broad is the way that leads to destruction, and many there be which go in there. Because straight is the gate and narrow is the way which leads us unto life and few there be that find it. **(Matthew 7:13-14 - NKJV).**

When you come to the gates in your path through this life on this rugged road, always go through the narrow one because that is the right one that leads to eternal life. As you journey, you will notice that many people are heading toward the wide gate, but that gate only leads to destruction.

You should also watch for false prophets as you travel this road to success. They will look good and appear attractive and persuasive, but they are wolves in sheep's clothing, waiting to deceive and devour. They can be identified by the lack of fruit in their lives; nothing at all can be seen. They are like barren trees; do not be deceived. This is where the spirit of discernment must be in full force. They may perform many good deeds, but when you examine their actions, you will see they are not doing the will of God. You might be tempted to be like them because they call on their God as their Lord, but it will not mean anything. Only those who discover God's will and remain obedient will find eternal life.

Watch out for people who lead you off the road. Do not think hanging around Christians or church members alone will prepare you for your journey. Some of the gates in the city of Jerusalem were so narrow that you could only go through one at a time, waiting your turn. You couldn't just walk along with the crowd; you had to make an intentional choice to go through the gate. The earth shows us that choice matters, actions and motives matter. Learning to follow Jesus, knowing Him as your Lord and Savior, and acknowledging Him as the God of your Father truly matters.

False prophets often seem nice; their words are carefully chosen and nicely seasoned. They seem trustworthy by their words, but if you are not watchful, their ideas and opinions can begin to creep into your life, influencing your thinking and creating doubt about this narrow way. Jesus gave us a very clear method of identifying false prophets. What does He say? You are to look at the life of the person. Just observe it and compare it to a tree. Can you see healthy, tasty fruits? Can you see others being nourished by them? Or does their life produce a crop of lies, immorality, and greed? Ultimately, the final word is about God's judgment and what Jesus declared on that day.

Jesus warns people about doing remarkable things in His name while not knowing Him personally. They may perform charitable deeds and claim to offer faithful services, but their actions are not genuine. Pretending to be good is not, by itself, an indicator of whether someone belongs to Jesus. As we continue traveling on this road of life and trusting God on our faith journey, we should understand that it is not just about holding on to the steering wheel and hoping for the best. We need to be aware of the dangers that can easily sidetrack us, leading us off the right path while deceiving us into thinking we are doing just fine.

We need to be vigilant and willing to follow the right path no matter what. That commitment will ultimately bring us joy in this life and eternal life with Jesus. What counts the most is not only knowing Jesus but also ensuring that He knows us.

Chapter 9

Guiding Signs on the Road to Success

My husband drives when we go places, allowing me to observe the road signs. I can apply spiritual applications to the different road signs you will encounter on the road to success.

Observe these signs as they are important for safety on this journey. Proceed carefully.

Some of the road signs on this road to success are as follows:

- One way.
- Overtaking is prohibited.
- Be prepared to stop.
- Stop, look, and listen for the still small voice.
- Proceed with caution.
- Narrow bridges. Remember, narrow is the way that leads to destruction.
- Go timely; the race is not for the swift.
- Speed trap. Proceed cautiously.
- Be careful for nothing.
- Do not detour!
- Be careful of the large gates.

- Look out for false prophets.
- Abide by God's will.
- Do not judge each other.
- Observe speed limits.
- Curves ahead.
- Dangerous, icy, slippery roads.
- Road work in progress.
- Ensure that you are doing God's will.

ONE WAY

A highway shall be there, and a road, and it shall be called the Highway of Holiness. The unclean shall not pass over it, but it shall be for others. Whoever walks the road, although a fool, shall not go astray. (Isaiah 35:8 – NKJV).

The road signs are explained, just be in obedience to the recommendations. It will pay off in the end.

It is dangerous if you go the wrong way. The Bible clearly states that there is only one way to heaven: believing in the Lord Jesus and accepting the gift of salvation He offers to anyone who believes by faith in God's Word (see **John 3:16, 14:16).**

It is in our best interest to accept the gift of Jesus that He offers. Otherwise, there is a danger of disobeying the road signs on this pathway, which will only allow you to end up in a horrific place called hell. It is my sincere wish that you will choose Jesus, who is the way, truth, and life.

UNDER CONSTRUCTION

When we see the sign "construction work ahead," it usually means we should be prepared to exercise patience and look out for disruptions.

Children of God should always be in the process of being shaped into the likeness of Christ, and we should continue until we meet God face to face. Christians need to be patient with themselves as well as with others, always remembering that this journey requires an abundance of caution.

We all experience trials and temptations, but these are to make us stronger and to be more like Christ. While we are under construction, we can see our growth, and the road will become more enjoyable and meaningful as the construction is complete.

"Under Construction" means God is not through with us yet. He is still molding us in His likeness and image. During this moment God holds us over in the "Potter's House." He is the Potter, and do not forget we are the clay, so His responsibility is to shape us into His image **(see Jeremiah 18:1-6).**

In the same way, as the potter skillfully shapes clay, God actively works in our lives, guiding our experiences and choices to form our character and purpose. This process can involve challenges and trials that help grow our faith, patience, and resilience, ultimately refining us to reflect His qualities more closely. Be aware that God has a specific plan for each of our lives, crafting our unique identities and destinies according to His will. God transforms our hearts and minds through His will and the Holy Spirit, aligning our desires and actions with His nature. Even when we stray or become flawed, God can reshape and restore us, illustrating His grace and mercy. Through these processes, we gradually conform to the image of Christ, reflecting His love, character, and holiness in the world.

When we accept salvation, God keeps working on us, fashioning us in the image of His Son **(see Romans 8:29)** until we are accepted in His presence in glory, where we will be finally perfected and made complete **(see 1 Corinthians 15:51-54)**. This requires patience on both our part and God's part.

God's patience with me is one thing I cherish, and I am eternally thankful. There will be challenges and inconveniences as we grow and learn in the process of maturing in Christ. Prepare for the reshaping of our lives from our loving God.

YIELD

This road sign indicates that we do not have the right of way, so we must wait and let someone else go first. Paul exhorts us, *"And do not*

present your members as an instrument of unrighteousness to sin but present yourselves to God as being alive from the dead, and your members as instruments of righteousness to God." (Romans 6:13 – NKJV). The moment we decide to walk with God, He should have the first place in our lives.

We should learn to wait on Him and give up the control of our hearts to Him. We must yield ourselves to the tender embrace of God and allow faith to take hold of the Word. Ensure your soul is completely anchored in God and lean on Jesus' strong arm; there no tempest can harm. We should remember that He knows what is best for us, so we should trust His perfect way **(see Psalm 18:30).**

STOP

The stop sign is self-explanatory. It simply means STOP. The stop sign does not mean slow down and look to see if anyone is watching, but this is when God tells us the things He wants us to stop doing:

— STOP loving the world and its allure (see 1 John 2:15).
— STOP acting like heathens (see Ephesians 4:17).
— STOP being selfish (see Philippians 2:3).
— STOP worrying (see Philippians 4:6).
— STOP talking trash (see Ephesians 5:29).
— STOP grieving the Holy Spirit (see Ephesians 5:30).

— STOP lying (see Ephesians 5:25).

These things are not only suggestions. We are sometimes tempted to ensure no one is watching; if not, we quickly indulge or break the STOP sign. This is treading on dangerous grounds. God is always watching us. His unseen eyes are always fixed on His children. Remember, there are consequences for every behavior.

DON'T ENTER. WRONG WAY

This is a warning not to go down a particular road because there is danger ahead, and disobeying this sign will not benefit us. God tells us the things we should stay away from.

For example, He says to avoid **Fornication:** which is sex outside of marriage (see 1 **Corinthians 10:13**). In the biblical context, God defines marriage as a sacred union between one man and one woman, intended to be a life-long commitment. It is viewed as a covenant reflecting a deep binding promise before God.

Another warning from God is about **idolatry:** Worshipping other gods or putting anything above God is a major sin, as it breaks the fundamental relationship between God and His followers **(see Exodus 20:3–5).**

Murder: Taking an innocent life is condemned, as human life is sacred in the eyes of God (see **Exodus 20:13**).

Lying and bearing false witness: Dishonesty harms relationships and society, and God calls for truthfulness (see Exodus 20:16).

Coveting: Desiring what belongs to others, whether their possessions or relationships, lead to envy and discontent (see **Exodus 20:17**).

These things are viewed as acts that not only harm the individual but also disrupt the harmony between them.

God will not accept anything less than what He states in His Word. I implore you to abide by God's rules.

OVERTAKING PROHIBITED

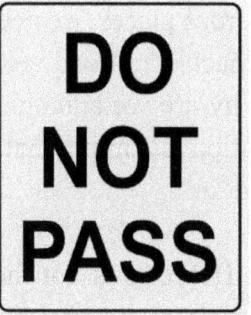

No matter how hard we try, we cannot rush through this journey of life. Impatience is a forbidden practice. We should use our spiritual strength and not our spirituality to enhance our ego or false identities. Let us not get angry or frustrated; instead, we should surrender our will and ways to God and take things in strides, depending on God to take us through this journey in His timing. Take it easy; be a spiritual tourist. Just enjoy the journey; enjoy your experience, observe the different areas on the road, and travel steadily to safety.

STOP, LOOK, AND LISTEN

Therefore, we must give more earnest heed to the things we have heard, lest we drift away. For if the word spoken through angels proved steadfast, and every transgression and disobedience received a just reward, how shall we escape if we neglect so great a salvation, which at the first began to be spoken by the Lord, and was confirmed to us by those who heard Him, God also bearing witness both with signs and wonders, with various miracles, and gifts of the Holy Spirit, according to His own will? **(Hebrews 2:1-4 – NKJV)**.

When we approach dangerous places, we need to stop and listen. What do we do when we approach a railroad crossing in normal life? We stop, look, and listen. Why are we admonishing you to do this? We need to find out if a situation is coming that can destroy us or if there is imminent danger ahead.

The danger described in Hebrews is not the danger of an oncoming physical train but of faltering on the Christian path and slipping away from Jesus. It is very easy for you to lay carelessly and wake up finding you are no longer a Christian. The first part of the scripture refers to that as drifting away.

I went to the beach, in the water, enjoying myself riding the waves and enjoying family and friends until, suddenly, I realized I had drifted away from where I first started. When I looked, I could not even see the blue and red beach umbrella my family rented for shade from the sun. If you have had that experience, you will agree that you might be lucky enough to see something that will allow you to figure out where that umbrella was, or if you have drifted too far, you end up being lost by not paying attention. Sometimes, you might find yourself with friends who pull you down, and as long as you go with them, they eventually become more important than your faith in God.

Hebrews 2:1-4 warns us not to drift from our faith. It counsels us to examine our lives frequently and see where we stand. This way, we will remain in close contact with the Lord. We need to understand that it doesn't matter how experienced we think we are, we should strive to remain faithful to the Lord. Drifting is real, so don't be fooled; it happens to persons we would look at as strong Christians. Drifting is such a discrete act. It happened slowly, so you will not feel that distress during the process. We find ourselves in different situations, sometimes being persecuted, lied to, and ridiculed, that sometimes drives us to wander away from the straight and narrow way. Many different circumstances are responsible for persons drifting away from God. For some people, the love and greed of money become their god, and they drift from the real path. That is just one of the many things.

Never allow anything or anyone to become more important than your faith in God, more important than your conscience, and more important than your integrity. It is a fact that drifting happens on this path to success, so we should stop, look, and listen to that still small voice of God.

PROCEED WITH CAUTION

"Proceed With Caution" can have many different meanings on this Christian pathway. This type of warning suggests that danger is imminent; there is a possibility of experiencing difficulties. Road signs are not installed as decorations but to let people know the possibilities of challenges and danger on the path. 'Proceed With Caution' signs don't indicate that we should stop or turn around when we become disturbed in spirit. It is a sign of warning from God that something is going wrong. The best remedy during these times is to seek God's direction, spend time with Him, and ask the Holy Spirit to intervene and be your guide. You cannot depend on your mind and emotions to keep you during this intricate moment. Continue to seek God's will, and He will direct you on the right path.

NARROW BRIDGE

In Christianity, the narrowest path refers to the path to eternal life. This is a difficult path, and very few people can go there. This path, according to Jesus, requires much effort and focus. I need to remind you that Jesus Himself is the gate. He is that gate to the sheepfold. This provides protection and boundaries for His flock, which He loves and cares for so well.

Jesus made it clear that the way to eternal life is restricted to just one avenue, and that is through Christ, but small is the gate, and narrow is the road that leads to life, and only a few find it. We all stand at our spiritual crossroads, and there are two paths in front of us: the wide path leads to hell and the second narrow path leads to life eternal in heaven. You need to make a choice **(see Matthew 7:14).**

SLOW DOWN

Ecclesiastes 9:11 states that the race is not for the swift. This has several Christian interpretations, including the divine favor of God. God is so kind; He gives success to people who are not the smartest, strongest, or best-looking. God sends the rain on the just as well as on the unjust (see Matthew 5:45). People must stop thinking they can leave God out and succeed on their own. You cannot make it if you leave God out of the room and try to rely on your strength. We need to release our attachment to self, and constantly seek God's protection, guidance, and help. You do not have to worry about your strength and ability; lean on a faithful God of grace. Rely on His support; He is

forever true. The Word of God exhorts us in **Philippians 4:6,** *"Be anxious for nothing, but in everything by prayer and supplication let your request be known to God." (NLJV).*

SPEED TRAP

Because of God's love for His children, He goes slowly and timely with us on our journey. God is love, and because He is love, He makes sure He spends time with us to ensure our safety on the journey with Him.

We need to surrender our ego. God's speed is different from the technological kind of speed to which we are accustomed. The speed of His love is a spiritual converging experience. This extends to the depth of our lives, whether anyone takes notice or not. When God walks with us, we have the time to see things from different perspectives, think more deeply, and get the chance to sort ourselves out and have more time to get away from jumbled thinking. Let us continue to trust God on this journey and enjoy a timely walk with him.

Our daily prayer; say this aloud as you read:

Lord, thank You for walking with me today. Help me to trust Your timing and guidance in every step I take. Strengthen my faith and lead me in Your ways so I may honor You in all I do. Grant me peace and patience, as I move forward with You, knowing You are with me in every moment, in Jesus' name. Amen.

BE CAREFUL FOR NOTHING

The Christian path requires careful attention and caution as it can be easy to stray from God's will or be led astray by worldly distractions. The Bible warns us to be vigilant and stay true to the faith.

In 1 Peter 5:8, we are reminded to be alert. *"Be alert and have a sober mind. Your enemy, the devil, prowls around like a roaring lion looking for someone to devour."*

Christians should learn that God uses our circumstances for His glory our growth, and refinement. God is always in control and possesses all power and authority. Instead of being worried, we should call for a posture of trust in God. As believers, we are encouraged to let go of worries and fears, recognizing that excessive anxiety can hinder our peace and faith.

Philippians 4:6 emphasizes the importance of prayer and supplication. Instead of worrying, we should bring our concerns to God and seek His guidance and support. It also encourages a mindset of thankfulness, which can help shift focus away from anxiety toward God's goodness.

"Be careful for nothing" encourages believers to rely on prayer and faith rather than succumbing to anxiety.

REST AREA

The "rest area" in natural life is where truck drivers and other drivers stop to be refreshed on a journey. This is where you can stop and rest from the stress of driving for a few minutes, have peace and refreshment, and enjoy your fellowship with other travelers.

God promises that a final resting place in heaven is reserved for the faithful. Our journey here on this earth can be challenging, but if we remain faithful, an eternal rest will be ours; it is forever. Sometimes, when earthly distractions get out of hand, we automatically become distracted, causing us to lose our way to the pearly gates where we will rest and find relief from this world and all its heartaches. If we remain faithful, and know Jesus as our savior, we will have peace, refreshment, and a glorious union with those believers who have gone on ahead of us, awaiting the resurrection. He is preparing a place called heaven for us, so make your reservation **(see John 14:1-2).**

There are different lights to encounter on this road to success.

RED LIGHT

Ignoring the spiritual red lights on the road to success can lead to several spiritual dangers. You can have a loss of direction. Disregarding red lights can lead you away from God—away from God's intended path—causing confusion and misalignment with His will. Pushing through hardship without seeking God's guidance and running a red light can result in exhaustion, both physically, and spiritually, and can eventually cause a major collision that could be fatal.

In pursuing success on this road, one may compromise on principles or ethics, leading to actions that conflict with one's faith. If you ignore the spiritual warnings of this red light, you can foster a sense of independence from the community, making it easier for you to stray from your faith. Recognizing and responding to spiritual red lights is crucial for maintaining an extremely healthy, balanced relationship with God while you trod this journey.

YELLOW LIGHT

In the secular world, a yellow light means to slow down and wait because the light will soon turn red. Flashing yellow lights means be careful by slowing down. In this spiritual walk, you should pay attention to your yellow lights and be alert for the red light.

AMBER LIGHT

When amber is on by itself, it means to stop until it is safe to go. Flashing amber means to proceed with care if the road is clear, giving way to pedestrians and other vehicles.

In the spiritual world, you need to pay attention to your amber light. Be very mindful of the consequences of ignoring the amber light. This often represents transition and change, guiding you through periods of growth and personal development. This light can enhance your intuition and insight, helping you recognize important lessons and messages in your experience.

GREEN LIGHT

In the secular world, this green light means to go and give permission to drivers and pedestrians to proceed. It is the same on the spiritual road of life; pay attention to your green light and what it signifies.

Green has always been a symbol of holiness, goodness, knowledge, wisdom, grace, hope, and God's revelation. God is not just a light; He is the light. The all-true light comes from Him. At the beginning of time, He created light to dispel darkness; the darkness and chaos subdued under a light is the source of goodness.

An ultimate reality is that God sets up traffic lights along our path. The Holy Bible clearly shows and encourages us to pay attention to the lights to have a successful journey. There would be so many tragic accidents on this Christian path if it were not for these lights. Many Christians ignore and even forget to acknowledge them. They refuse to pay attention to these major lights and end up getting into serious accidents. The lights are assigned to show the right of way to conflicting traffic movements at an intersection.

The green light on the road to success often symbolizes progress, permission, or moving forward. In the context of hardship, it could represent moments of clarity, opportunity, or breakthrough that arise after overcoming obstacles. Even when faced with difficulty, the green light reminds you that the journey is still moving forward and that success is within reach despite the challenges. It is a signal to keep going.

We must respect the instructions given by the Almighty. These lights with assorted colors have a spectacular and distinct meaning, triggering specific reactions from drivers and pedestrians. As I mentioned before, we sometimes check to see if anyone is watching before we do the right thing, but we should not deceive ourselves because God's eyes are watching us. There will be a harvest of what we have sown (see **Galatians 6:7**). You are not free from the consequences of your choice. Follow the instructions of the lights and continue to make your journey safe.

Important Rules of the Road **(see Exodus 20:2-17, Deuteronomy 5:6-21 and Exodus 34:11-26).**

- Love the Lord with all your heart and with all your might **(see Deuteronomy 6:5).**
- If you love Me, keep My commandments **(see John 14:15).**

- Therefore, whatever you want men to do to you, do also to them **(see Matthew 7:12)**.
- Do not be overcome by evil but overcome evil with good **(see Romans 12:21)**.
- Be steadfast and unmovable, always abounding in the work of the Lord. For you know that your labor will not be in vain **(see 1 Corinthians 15:58)**.
- Thou shall have no other gods before me **(see Exodus 20:3-5)**.
- Thou shall not take the name of the Lord in vain **(see Exodus 20:7)**.
- Remember the Sabbath day to keep it holy **(see Exodus 20:8)**.
- Honor your father and mother so that your days may be long **(see Exodus 20:12)**.
- Thou shall not kill **(see Exodus 20:13)**.
- Thou shall not commit adultery **(see Exodus 20:14)**.
- Thou shall not steal **(see Exodus 20:15)**.

IT IS IMPORTANT TO REMEMBER

Jeremiah 31:21a says, *"Set up signposts, make landmarks;" (NKJV)*.

Get a good roadmap and study the road conditions.

Enter through the narrow gate, for broad is the road that leads to destruction; many enter through it. But small is the gate, and narrow is the road that leads to life, and only a few find it (see Matthew **7:13-23)**.

God preserves our going out and coming in from this time forth and even forevermore. He will get us to our destination safely. God's divine Word and His unfailing presence in our lives give us the safe directions we are to go. The most wonderful thing about God is that He can see our danger long before us. He will speak to us and advise us to turn around, stand still, wait for instructions, or move forward, whatever the case may be. He will inform us on time if we are nearing a dead end. Our only requirement is to listen to His voice and obey His commands.

Always remember, God knows what is best for us. Whenever danger is imminent, our father jumps before us and shields us from danger. This journey is tremendously beautiful because our heavenly Father never leaves us alone. He is always protecting us from unseen dangers. There are many challenges, but you should not fear anything if God is by your side. You will never fail on this journey with your master by your side.

Everyone's assignments are different. Even husbands and wives who become one flesh when joined in holy matrimony get individual and specific assignments from God. Friends, family, mothers, fathers, and siblings have their assignments. Everyone bears their responsibilities. We must pay attention, stay in our lane, never cross the yellow line, and do not try to push anyone off track.

And do not lead us into temptation but deliver us from the evil one. For Yours is the kingdom and the power and the glory forever. Amen. (Matthew 6:13 - NKJV).

We face temptations daily, but we are cautioned not to yield. A songwriter says it appropriately, *"Yield not to temptation, for yielding is sin; Each victory will help you, some other to win; fight valiantly onward, evil passions subdue; Look ever to Jesus, He will carry you through."*

Our lives should be saturated with love, grace, and total dependence on the Almighty. Some call Him Jesus; some say the Alpha and the

Omega, the Beginning and the End, the First and the Last, Lamb of God, Emmanuel, Savior, Chief Cornerstone, Refuge, Advocate, Chief Shepherd, Savior, Deliverer, Light of the World, Mediator, Redeemer, Rock, Counselor, Mighty God, Teacher, and the great I Am that I Am.

What a mighty God we serve. He is called by different names by different people.

We have different occupations, and I think with each profession, He can be represented.

- To the **Architect**, He is a builder, the chief cornerstone.
- To the **Baker,** He is the bread of life.
- To the **Cardiologist**, He searches the intents of our hearts.
- To the **Doctor,** He is a great physician, the balm in Gilead.
- To the **Electrician**, He is the light of the world.
- To the **Farmer**, He is the Lord of the harvest.
- To the **Geologist**, He is the rock of salvation.
- To the **Hairdresser**, He says He numbers every hair on our heads.
- To the **Illustrator**, He taught lessons to His followers through images of plants, vines, and seeds.
- To the **Jeweler,** there are twelve sacred gemstones of Revelation: jasper, chalcedony, emerald, sardonyx, sardius, chalcedony, sardius, beryl, topaz, chrysolite, jacinth, and amethyst.
- To the **Kitchen Assistant**, He prepares a table before us in the presence of our enemies.
- To the **Lawyer,** He is our advocate.
- To the **Meteorologist**, He calms the raging sea.
- To the **Nurse**, He binds the brokenhearted and sets those who are bound at liberty.

- To the **Optometrist**, God's eyes are always watching over us from the moment we are conceived to eternity.
- To the **Psychologist**, He is a wonderful counselor.
- To the **Quality Control Inspector**, He monitors us, checking to make sure we are meeting His standards and specifications. monitoring our everyday lives is one of His main duties.
- To the **Realtor**, He said for Himself "In my Father's house there are many mansions. If it were not so, I would have told you. I will prepare a place for you that where I am, there you will be also."
- To the **Surgeon**, He binds the brokenhearted and sets at liberty those who are bound.
- To the **Teacher,** He is our theological educator. He taught the twelve and taught the crowds as well.
- To the **Ultrasound Technician**, He makes sure our image of Him is clear, notes the abnormalities, and refers us to the Holy Spirit to work on any area that needs attention.
- To the **Veterinarian,** the cattle on a thousand hills are His. He knows every bird in the mountains and every living thing in the fields is His. If He were hungry, He would not tell you, because the earth and everything in it are His.
- To the **Writer**, He is the author and finisher of our faith.
- To the **X-ray Technician**, He knows us inside out. He knows every bone in our body, exactly how we were made, bit by bit, and how we were sculpted from nothing into something.
- To the **Youth Coordinator**, young man, I call upon you because ye are strong, and the Word of God abides in you (see 1 John 2:14).
- To the **Zoologist,** He is the conquering lion of the tribe of Judah.

I could keep on writing for endless pages about the different names of Jesus and how He relates even to our various professions. He means so much to me; I am sure you would say the same. Despite the mistakes I made, the wrong turns I had taken, and my faith in Him at times seemed to have been abandoned, He still journeyed on this road with me. His arms are always open, and He is ready and willing to help and meet me each time at my point of need. He is always there to lift me when I need Him most. He is there to do the same for you. He is a promise keeper. No matter how lonely, depressed, confused, rejected, and alone we feel, He is right there by our side. He remains unfailing, ever-loving, ever-true, **omnipresent** (everywhere at the same time), **omniscient** (all-knowing, being aware of everything), **omnipotent** (all-powerful, having unlimited power).

When the storm of life starts raging, and the seas become rough, I have learned to trust Jesus, follow in obedience, and listen to His instructions. He is right there with you in the storms.

This road to success is sometimes very unpleasant. The pain, suffering, and hardships we sometimes encounter are hard to explain. These rough storms can help us see how much our anchor holds. Storms tell us where we are in God and where our faith stands. We should live by faith and not by sight. The storms allow God to work on our behalf, show up, and show off His capabilities.

Paul was falsely accused and imprisoned. He was transported by ship to Rome. During the storm, an angel appeared to Paul to let him know that he and everybody on board would be saved. What a consolation in that difficult time! The storms blew hard and blew the ship off course, which caused it to break up near the island of Malta. Because of God's protection, Paul finally arrived in Rome, having survived a storm, a shipwreck, and even a snake bite (see **Acts 27).**

The next night, the Lord stood by Paul and told him to be brave. He had already told people in Jerusalem about Jesus, so he was commissioned to do the same in Rome. The Roman Centurion was Julius. He delivered this prisoner and would have been required to guard him with his life. Julius treated Paul kindly and even allowed him to see his friends when the ship stopped at the first port. The stormy weather meant the boat would not take a direct route, so the pilot sailed on the east and south sides of Crete and took shelter in a southern port called Fair Havens. In **Acts 27:9,** Luke writes that it was now after the Fast, which was the Jewish Day of Atonement held in September or October. There was no way for the ship to take refuge for the winter. Paul warned the centurion to stay in Fairhaven; Julius listened to the ship's pilot. The decision was made to try to sail further along the southern coast to Crete and, in the winter, to the more suitable port of Phoenix. The ship never made it. Storms pushed it well off course and further into the Mediterranean.

The Mediterranean Sea can be very rough and dangerous. The situation became so grave and desperate that the cargo was eventually thrown overboard to stay afloat. After receiving the Lord's message, Paul was able to tell everyone on board that all lives would be spared. This time, they listened to him. When the ship hit a sandbar and began to break up, all 276 passengers and crew on board made it safely to shore by swimming or floating in on boards from the same broken ship. It went just as Paul said **(see Acts 28).** This allowed Paul to gain a lot of respect among the crew, but the Islanders were also impressed by him when he survived a snake bite from a snake that emerged from some firewood on the beach **(see Acts 28:3-6)**.

After healing the father of one of the chief officers on the island, people began to bring others to Paul to be healed. After three months on the island and the stormy winter had passed, Paul's group boarded another ship and made their way to Rome. The people of Malta provided all the provisions they needed for that journey. On reaching Rome, Paul was allowed to live by himself with a soldier protecting him (see **Acts 12**). It is good to note the providence of God in protecting Paul as he made his way to Rome.

Paul was:

- protected from angry men.
- whisked away by night when there was a plot against him.
- treated with kindness by a centurion who guarded his life.
- given special treatment while being held as a prisoner in Herod's Palace.
- heard when the crew listened to him on an Egyptian ship.
- respected by the Islanders and the chief Roman official of Malta.
- provided with supplies for the remainder of his journey.

When the storms of life face you, it takes God alone to see you through. Popularity, money, and success are worthless and useless during this period. When you face the storms of life, cling to Jesus, who is your friend and your only hope.

That by two immutable things, in which it is impossible for God to lie, we might have strong consolation, who have fled for refuge to lay hold of the hope set before us. This hope we have as an anchor of the soul, both sure and steadfast, and which enters the Presence behind the veil, where the forerunner has entered for us, even Jesus, having become High Priest forever according to the order of Melchizedek. **(Hebrews 6:18-20 – NKJV).**

Do you give thanks for God's provisions when you are at a business luncheon? Do you bow your heads and thank the Lord for your blessings in front of your friends? Is this what we should always do, particularly when God has us in a storm? Can you praise Him while you are in your storm?

A storm in a Christian's life is like a megaphone. The world is watching to see how you are going to respond. Be bold, share your faith, and let others know where your faith lies. Yeah!!! we should all be encouraged. Storms are real on this journey to success. If you have not faced a storm, just keep on living; the storm will come. The big question is, *"Where does your faith lie?"* The Bible makes it truly clear that one day, perhaps soon, when all the storms have passed, believers will arrive at a bay with a sandy beach, a place that has been prepared for them. The Bible calls this place "Paradise," and everyone who arrives there will once and forever be safe.

In John 16:22, Jesus said, *"So with you: Now is your time of grief, but I will see you again and you will rejoice, and no one will take away your joy." (NIV).*

When we who are in Christ arrive in heaven, all our storms will have already passed away; all our questions will be answered. Amen. Just remember that while the storms are raging, we are still waiting for the showers of blessings that we are sure will come. The seas might be rough and variable but with Christ in the vessel, we will smile at the storm.

Giving up is not an option. Have courage and keep riding on the billows for home. The songwriter says, *"Firmly stand for God, in the world's mad strife. Tho' the bleak winds roar, and the waves beat high; 'Tis the Rock alone giveth strength and life, When the hosts of sin are high."*

Chapter 10

The Life of a Soldier Compared to the Road to Success Paved With Hardships

A soldier in the army can be described as a disciplined and trained individual who serves in a military organization tasked with defending their country and maintaining peace. For conducting various operations and missions, soldiers are typically characterized by their commitment to duty, teamwork, and physical fitness, which are enhanced by a strict code of conduct. They are often trained in combat skills, survival tactics, and specialized areas such as logistics, communications, or engineering. Soldiers also embody values such as courage, loyalty, integrity, and selfishness and are willing to make personal sacrifices for the greater good of their country and comrades.

In Christian theology, God calls believers to be faithful soldiers of the cross as a metaphor for living out their faith with dedication, discipline, and perseverance. Much like a soldier in service for their country, the metaphor emphasizes that Christians are engaged in a spiritual battle that requires steadfastness, commitment, and reliance on God's strength.

God is depending on us because we are indeed soldiers of the cross. In Philippians 2:25 and Philemon 1:2, Paul describes fellow Christians as "Fellow soldiers." The image of a soldier is also used in 2 Timothy 2:3-4 as a metaphor for courage, loyalty, and dedication.

"You, therefore, must endure hardship as a good soldier of Jesus Christ. No one engaged in warfare entangles himself with the affairs of this life, that he may please him who enlisted him as a soldier." (2 Timothy 2:3-4 - NKJV).

God expects us to be faced with challenging circumstances, but He makes adequate provision for us to overcome these trials and come out victoriously. The command *"to suffer hardship"* is a direct command. No soldier on active duty has any time to entangle himself in the affairs of everyday life. If you ask a soldier about hardship, he will tell you that hardship is a part of the journey. It is not just about physical challenges but mental and emotional endurance too. You learn to push through pain, fatigue, and fear because you know your mission and your comrades depend on you. Hardship teaches you resilience and, in the end, it strengthens your character and your resolve.

Paul called Timothy to accompany him in the common suffering. If you examine Paul's life, you would hesitate to join him in his suffering; however, the cause for which he lived drew many others to Christ. People are drawn to the common suffering of military life because of the "cause." A soldier knows and would understand what Paul is talking about here; they do not take the call to join the military lightly. In the everyday life of suffering, people who don't understand what hardship is are ready to quit with the first challenge. Unlike a soldier who knows what that means, it makes them more determined to commit. A good soldier commits without the option of quitting.

Cadets and military men and women know that they live a lifestyle that is different from the world or what we call civilians. Civilians often misunderstand or avoid these people because they live by a different system. A good soldier does not get entangled in the affairs of civilian life. The life of a follower of Christ is also different from the life of the world. The purpose and goals are different; therefore, the system of life in which they live is also different. If a disciple's purpose is to advance the kingdom of God, they cannot live focused on advancing their kingdom. What do you think motivates a soldier to suffer hardships and avoid things that will distract them from being a good soldier? They embrace the seven core values of the US Army, which are loyalty, duty, respect, self-service, honor, integrity, and personal courage.

A soldier's greatest motivation to join and serve in the army can vary based on personal values, experiences, and goals. Some common motivations include:

1. **Patriotism and duty**: Many soldiers feel a deep sense of loyalty to their country and are driven by a desire to serve and protect their nation.

2. **Camaraderie and brotherhood:** The bond formed with fellow soldiers is often a powerful motivator. The sense of belonging to a team with a shared mission can provide purpose and support.
3. **Personal growth and discipline:** The military offers opportunities for personal development, including physical fitness, leadership skills, and resilience. Some joined the army to challenge themselves and develop traits that will serve them in life.
4. **Career and stability**: The military can provide steady employment benefits and career advancement opportunities, which can appeal to individuals seeking job security or a structured career path.
5. **Adventure and travel**: The promise of travel, exposure to new cultures, and the adventure of serving in various parts of the world are other major attractions for many recruits.
6. **Family legacy:** For some, joining the military is a family tradition, and they may feel motivated to continue a legacy of service passed down through the generations.
7. **A sense of honor and sacrifice**: The desire to make a meaningful contribution, often at great personal cost, can serve as a strong motivating factor. Many soldiers see their service as a way to give back and to protect others, especially loved ones or vulnerable populations.
8. **Financial incentives**: Some are motivated by financial benefits such as signing bonuses, education assistance, and health coverage.

In many cases, these motivations are not mutually exclusive, and the soldier's drive may stem from a combination of factors.

Soldiers, in general, will tell you that they suffer much hardship in reaching higher ranks but remain committed to the cause. They bear an exceptional understanding that includes both their hearts and hands. How will you respond to your heavenly Commander in the army of God? If you know the love and power of the Commander, Jesus Christ, I imagine you will entrust your life to Him and ask the Father in heaven, *"What is my mission?"* or *"What will You have me to do?"*

Paul gives an account of all the sufferings he endured for Christ (**see 2 Corinthians 11:23-28**). He told the church to bring glory to God. He emphasizes that God will grant him the grace to endure the suffering. Paul describes his experience as a minister of Christ and a soldier of the cross. Traveling on this journey to success, we need to make sure we have a made-up mind to continue to the end; we are called soldiers. We need to remain fit for battle because we can be called at any time for service. Soldiers in secular military service are called to continue serving through the most challenging times.

As soldiers of Christ, we must possess special characteristics. Let us examine some of these qualities or characteristics:

- **Loyalty:** We should bear true faith and allegiance to God as fellow soldiers of Christ.
- **Commitment to duty:** You are expected to carry out the duty entrusted to you and fulfill your obligations.
- **Respect:** Christians can create a respectful and loving environment where mutual respect and unity flourish in the body of Christ.
- **Selfless service:** As a faithful servant, you should put the welfare of the saints and fellow soldiers before your own.
- **Honor:** Remember to give honor where honor is due.
- **Integrity:** As a soldier of the cross, you must live and respect the call of Christ on your life.
- **Personal courage:** Personal courage is important to have; always try to encourage yourself in the Lord.

A good soldier of Jesus Christ should not be distracted by everything in their life. All you should be concerned about is keeping focused and representing the Lord Jesus Christ. If you leave yourself careless and distracted, you are putting yourself in the way of being hit by the fiery darts of the wicked one. A true soldier is willing to fight the fight and exhibit the unfaltering focus of fighting to win. This mindset keeps the purpose in our mandate.

As a true soldier, you will have to live up to the values of Christ.

DISPLAY INTEGRITY

A Christian soldier should display integrity by living out biblical values in every aspect of their life. Integrity should be demonstrated by a Christian soldier's respect for their commanding officer who could be their religious leader, as well as respect for their fellow Christians. This respect reflects their ultimate reverence for God's authority (see **Romans 13:1-2**). You should remain faithful and live up to the standards put forth in the Word of God: courage, discipline, loyalty, and obedience.

In battle, soldiers wear protected gear to safeguard themselves from physical harm and ensure their readiness for the challenges they might encounter. Their gear is often referred to as "combat gear" or "load out." This is designed to provide essential protection, functionality, and readiness in a variety of combat or operational environments. The gear includes several components, each serving a critical role in ensuring the soldier's safety, mobility, and effectiveness.

Christian soldiers—metaphorically speaking—are those who follow Christ and navigate life's challenges. There is a parallel in how they should prepare for their spiritual battle. In **Ephesians 6:10-18**, the apostle Paul speaks of the armor of God that equips believers to withstand the trials, temptations, and hardships that come with living a righteous life in a fallen world. The spiritual armor is not physical but is the powerful protective framework for the Christians' journey.

The armor of God includes:

1. **Belt of Truth**: Just as soldiers wear belts to secure their armor and ensure everything stays in place, Christians are to gird themselves with truth. Truth holds everything together and provides clarity in a world full of lies and deceit.
2. **Breastplate of righteousness**: A breastplate protects vital organs in battle, especially the heart. Similarly, righteousness guards the Christian heart from sin and corruption, ensuring their motives, decisions, and actions align with God's will.
3. **Shoes of the gospel of peace**: Soldiers need sturdy boots to travel long distances, endure harsh terrains, and stand firm in battle. Christians are called to have their feet shod with the preparation of the gospel of peace, meaning they must be prepared to spread their message of peace and stand firm in their faith no matter the challenges they encounter.
4. **Shield of faith:** Just as a soldier uses a shield to block arrows and attacks, Christians must hold up the shield of faith to deflect the fiery darts of doubt, fear, and temptation that come from the enemy. Faith acts as a defense against life's trials.
5. **Helmet of salvation:** A helmet protects the head, and similarly, salvation is the assurance that protects the Christian mind from despair and confusion. The certainty of eternal life provides clarity and confidence amid adversity.
6. **Sword of the Spirit**: A soldier's sword is his/her weapon of choice. For Christians, the sword is the Word of God, which can counter lies, stand against temptation, and advance God's kingdom.
7. **Prayer:** Christians are to pray in the Spirit on all occasions. Prayer is a vital communication link with the Commander—

who is God—ensuring soldiers stay in touch with their source of strength and direction.

Just as a soldier's gear is carefully chosen, fitted, and worn for maximum protection and effectiveness, Christians must intentionally put on the armor of God. Much like a battlefield, the road to success is filled with struggles, obstacles, and hardships, but by being equipped with the proper spiritual armor, Christians can stand firm, fight with strength, and confidently march toward the reward God has prepared for them.

Christians must prepare themselves with the armor of God to face spiritual battles in life through truth, righteousness, peace, faith, salvation, the Word of God, and prayer. We are equipped to overcome the hardships on our journey to success. We must conduct ourselves wisely and lead by example. The journey is great and challenging, but we are expected to walk with God faithfully and humbly in every aspect of our lives.

A true soldier knows what it means to surrender their lives to God and God alone. Christian soldiers should rest completely and securely in the arms of Jesus. The assurance of God's presence and power will help us overcome the seen and unseen heartaches and trials.

NOTES

_____

_____

_____

_____

_____

Chapter 11

The Life of a Sailor Compared to the Road to Success Paved With Hardships

A sailor is typically depicted as a resolute and adventurous individual who works on ships, navigating the sea and ensuring safe passage. They often wear practical clothing suited for the ocean, such as a navy blue uniform, waterproof gear, and sturdy boots. Sailors are skilled in various tasks, including operating and navigation equipment, managing sails, and rigging to harness wind effectively for propulsion. They also conduct drills to manage emergencies and ensure compliance with maritime regulations. They possess a powerful sense of teamwork and often form close bonds with fellow crew members during long voyages. The life of a sailor is marked by resilience and adaptability.

Like a sailor traveling out there at sea, a believer will come across so many difficult and uncontrollable situations during which the intricacies of the journey surface. A sailor out there at sea can tell you that sailing involves a kind of *"Loving up or romancing with the wind."* The wind is observed as it is, and the sailor will have to adapt to it, learn to maneuver around it, and understand its vicissitudes. He has to adapt to the harsh, rough winds and love up on whatever the wind dictates.

A sailor will tell you that when he "catches" the wind, the boat then speeds along as the sails play their part. The sails are often made of bright colors and light fabric—usually nylon—and are attached at three points. They can be designed to perform best as either a reaching or running spinnaker. They would make this slick sound in the water; other times, there were thrilling and daring times when the spinnaker, a sail made specifically for sailing off the wind, showed off its ability to sail deep.

In our spiritual walk on the road to success, we have difficult days and times when the winds become contrary, and there are demanding times with the winds. One cannot control the wind but has no choice but to accept it as it is; accept, embrace it, and work with what comes our way. To live in the world is a challenge, and we sometimes wish we could change things in this world and fix them the way we think they should be or how they would have us go, but we just cannot. I exhort you to hold on to the promises of God. He has the key to our victory. Remember, our total victory is in the hands of a noticeably big, able God.

The good sailor accepts that a good, strong breeze can suddenly grow calm, only to frighteningly stir again. This happens mostly on sultry summer days. When the prevailing winds are less evident, the strength and direction of the winds can be very local.

As pilgrims, sojourners, and sailors on life's sea, we need to be aware of sudden storms and rough, dangerous waters, so it is important to monitor and listen to heaven's weather reports. Be ready to adjust your plans if conditions change. Carry your life jacket, which is the Word of God. Be prepared for inclement weather, and always think of a safety plan. Do not take any extra baggage on this voyage. The Word of God exhorts us in Hebrews 12:1, *"Therefore, since we are surrounded by such a great cloud of witnesses, let us throw off everything that hinders, and the sin that so easily entangles; And let us run with perseverance, the race marked out for us."* Read your Bible—which is your road map—as it will give instructions for a safe journey.

The life of a Christian can be compared to the life of a sailor. A sailor on board the ship is expected to do what the captain orders. The captain, I believe, knows that the best way to ensure a sailor is out of trouble is to keep him occupied. So it is with the Christian journey: our Captain, Jesus, allows certain situations to face us. They challenge us on our journey. This will keep us on our knees and force us to constantly listen to the voice of God for orders. The Master instructs us what to always do, so you should keep listening to that voice that makes the difference.

We can use the sailboat to symbolize the Christian walk. The storm moves the boat by filling the sails with wind. In our Christian walk, the Holy Spirit empowers and gives us the courage to go on. On board a sailboat, sailors on deck duty operate the vessel and the deck equipment. They make up the deck crew and maintain all the parts of the ship. They must ensure that the ship is in good working order.

On the Christian's walk, the Holy Spirit is our constant guide. Sailing can be a very exhilarating journey. The wind dances and parades, infusing life into each adventure. A sailor's life lessons goes beyond the open sea as they often serve. This serves as a valuable metaphor for personal and professional growth.

A good sailor possesses good stamina and lots of perseverance. When the sea gets rough, he cannot decide whether to give up or jump off the boat, but he must sail through rough seas and uncontrollable winds and make it to shore. It is the same for the Christian walk, which calls for resilience, perseverance, and good stamina. These are the main keys to a successful walk with God. Perseverance and resilience are two must-have tools to walk on this challenging road to success. Interestingly, rough times in the Christian walk help us access and realize our degree or level of determination.

Fighting against all odds is an integral part of the success of this journey. Demonstrating perseverance and resilience in adverse situations helps shape our character and reveal what material we are made of. Traveling this journey requires displaying undisturbed attention, resourcefulness, anticipation, patience, and prioritization, which are essential ingredients and requirements for a progressive journey.

You will have to constantly renew your goals and work hard to achieve them accordingly. This journey is not a bed of roses but a long road to go; however, we must be brave, and with that determination, strong faith, and trust in God, we can hold on to the end. Jesus never promised that our road would be easy, neither did He tell us that it would always be sunshine. He never said it would always rain either. One thing He promised us is that He would always be with us through thick and thin, sunshine and rain, comfort and pain, on the mountain, down in the valley; just have confidence, He will journey with us always.

The anticipation and assurance of walking the streets of glory, the privilege to be able to tell redemption's story, combined with having the confidence that our Promise Keeper will be there with us to help us run through a troop, leap over the wall, and end the road victoriously should give us the strength we need to go through. We cannot allow ourselves to become slaves to fear. Make a special effort to eliminate the frequent doubts that tend to dampen our spirit.

Our daily prayer should be, *"Lord, lift me up and let me stand, by faith on Canyon's table land, a higher plane that I have found. Lord, plant my feet on higher ground."* Our heart should be fixed on making our walk a successful one. Our desires for earthly gains should be nowhere near us; we should have no desire to stay where doubts arise or fear dismay; though some may dwell where these abound, our aim should always be for higher ground. We will see many people branching off to side lanes and some nice, attractive paved roads, but all we should be aiming for is higher ground. We should be in the world, but not of this world (see John 17:16). The darts of the enemy will always be fired at us, but with God's help and protection, none will catch us or destroy us. I implore you to stay equipped.

Above all, taking the shield of faith, wherewith ye shall be able to quench all the fiery darts of the wicked. (Ephesians 6:16 - KJV).

Paul compares the dragon's attack to flaming arrows that can set ablaze anything that encounters it, such as doubt, fear, anger, guilt, loneliness, depression, and many more. The shield of faith extinguishes and destroys all these unwanted attachments. Fiery darts referred to Roman soldiers as they would soak their shields in water to prevent them from catching fire if hit by the enemy's arrows. What a blessing to the saints of Christ. A songwriter pends this line, *"He will hide me safely, hide me where no arm can e'er betide me; He will hide me in the shadow of his hands. Though he may send some affliction 'twill but make me long for home, for in love and not in anger, all His chastening will come."*

There is a consolation to rest; depend on God for comprehensive blood coverage. The good thing is that for all the bad situations, God turns whatever seems to harm us into everlasting joy. You are encouraged to be faithful even when things get hard. Storms rage high, and the fight gets wild at times, but remember that Jesus cares for our souls, and if He cares, nobody or nothing at all can harm us. He takes pleasure in caring for His children.

"For I know the thoughts that I think toward you, saith the Lord, thoughts of peace, and not of evil, to give you an expected end." (Jeremiah 29:11 – KJV).

Prophet Jeremiah wrote a letter to the Israelites during the time they were in exile in Babylon during the reign of King Nebuchadnezzar. He stated that God had a plan for His people, and He is capable of working through our various circumstances, making the outcome work for our good; He wants to prosper and give us hope. It can also be identified as a promise of hope to us. To succeed on this journey, we must be prepared to go through the process, however difficult it may seem.

Chapter 12

The Life of a Jeweler Compared to the Road to Success Paved With Hardships

The Christians' test, trials, and sanctification are referred to in the Bible as the purification of gold. Many of us love gold, but the process is severe. For gold to become pure, it must go through a powerful process. It is the same with the children of God. We must be refined and processed if we should come forth worthwhile or worth anything valuable.

Gold is purified by fire. The gold is melted, and as the impurities rise to the surface, it can be easily removed. All impurities must go. It is the same for our Christian journey. Trials come to mold us and make us into the direct image of God.

The Bible mentions gold numerous times. It is often associated with wealth, divine presence, purity, and perfection. Gold points us to King Jesus and His bride (the church). The testing of gold is analogous to faith and trials, but guess what? Genuine faith endures eternally. Despite the tedious tests we must go through, we need to remember that these trials are ordained to test the reality of our faith in the same way there is a process for purifying precious metals. Keep the faith, my friend! We will be like gold that has been appraised on fire. These trials will prove that your faith is still worth much more than gold. The Bible has several verses that mention God's refining process, including God as a refiner and purifier of silver.

For thou, O God, hast proved us: thou hast tried us, as silver is tried. (Psalm 66:10 – KJV).

And some of them of understanding shall fall, to try them, and to purge, and to make them white, even to the time of the end: because it is yet for a time appointed. (Daniel 11:35 – KJV).

Behold, I have refined thee, but not with silver; I have chosen thee in the furnace of affliction. (Isaiah 48:10 – KJV).

And I will bring the third part through the fire, and will refine them as silver is refined, and will try them as gold is tried: they shall call on my name, and I will hear them: I will say, It is my people: and they shall say, The Lord is my God. (Zechariah 13:19 – KJV).

1 Peter 1:7 says that your faith will be like gold and silver that has been evaluated in a fire. The refining process is a crucial part of our growth in God. It removes areas that are not beneficial to us. These are some of the things that the refining fire does:

- It strengthens us spiritually and builds our character.
- It sets people free from setbacks.
- It prepares people to keep promises.
- It gets rid of all impurities.
- This process is repeated until you are pure and clean, and the reflection of Christ can be evident. Just by looking at us, one can see the reflection of Christ in us.
- It prepares us for God's promises. God will refine people to prepare them to obtain His promise.
- It forces us to cooperate with God. When people cooperate with God's work, all impurities, like unbelief, pride, and selfishness, will surface so God can eradicate them. When repentance occurs, we become more like Christ.

It is such a rough but beautiful experience to be purged and purified through the trials and tribulations that God allows. When you are grieved by all of these, the genuineness of your faith is assessed and proven. One songwriter says, *"The hotter the battle, the sweeter the victory."* Another says, *"Wash me and purge me until I am lost in You."*

Refining is not punishment but a blessing and evidence that God loves you and works in your life. Biblically, gold is often portrayed as a symbol of God's majesty and glory. The pruning and refining process is used to deliver us from the very things that hold us back. The sole responsibility we have is to trust the process. If you do not even fully understand God's ways and timing, just remember that He is working things out for your good. When the feeling of discouragement comes, take it to the Lord in prayer.

God is never frustrated by our struggles, doubts, pains, or ill feelings that He permits. He has a way of addressing our various emotions. You need to dig deep into God's Word. Find the time each day to spend with God. God is bigger than any of the circumstances you face. Refrain from complaining and start looking for things to be grateful for. Be patient enough to wait on God for the answer. Nothing is more rewarding than trusting God, even in the most difficult times. Living at the mercy seat in prayer makes knowing God's plan for your life possible. Maintain an active habit of reading God's Word. Follow the command God puts on your heart. You must know God and trust Him totally with your life.

God has many plans for our lives, so we should place ourselves in His hands so He can make and mold us in His likeness. Our daily prayer should be, *"To be like Jesus, to be like Jesus, that's all I ask, to be like Him. All through life's journey, from earth to glory, one thing I ask is to be like Him."*

Jesus is our perfect example of love, compassion, and obedience to God. By following His teachings and actions, Christians can grow spiritually, reflect God's character, and fulfill their purpose of spreading His love and truth in the world. Imitating Jesus helps believers deepen their relationship with God and live out their faith in a way that brings glory to Him.

Chapter 13

The Life of a Baker Compares to the Road to Success Paved With Hardships

It can be remarkably interesting to draw a comparison between going through hardship in the pursuit of achievement and baking bread. Both tasks require a lot of effort and patience to reach a goal that includes distinct stages of change.

A good baker will tell you that when baking bread, you begin with some basic ingredients like water, flour, yeast, and salt. Each component must be fully combined. In the same way the dough must be worked upon and kneaded to develop the gluten and acquire the proper consistency, people must go through problems, setbacks, and personal growth to achieve success.

The dough resets and rises during the period of what is called the "proofing" phase. During this phase, things appear to move slowly. There are no shortcuts to this process. You have to wait for the process to be complete. It then goes in the closed oven under specified degrees of heat and specific timing. That bread is not called bread until the dough goes through that heat for the desired time of completion. When it is completed, the baker gets the satisfaction of a beautiful, delicious loaf of bread. Think about the process the dough goes through; it is pressed, kneaded, squeezed, placed under intense pressure, and put aside as if forgotten to achieve the required results. People also need time to see the fruits of their labor. As hoped for, the bread needs time to rise and take on a particular texture.

After this process, the dough is baked, and the results are amazing and complete. This phase is a coming together of all the hardships, difficulties, and tenacity. The pressure and the obstacles unite everything in a completely successful outcome.

In both situations, the procedure or the task incorporates pain and effort, but the end thereof can be very satisfying. There will be no success without hardship and persistence. Weathering the challenges to achieve positive results is the way to go.

Chapter 14

Life in the Medical Field Compared With the Road to Success Paved With Hardships

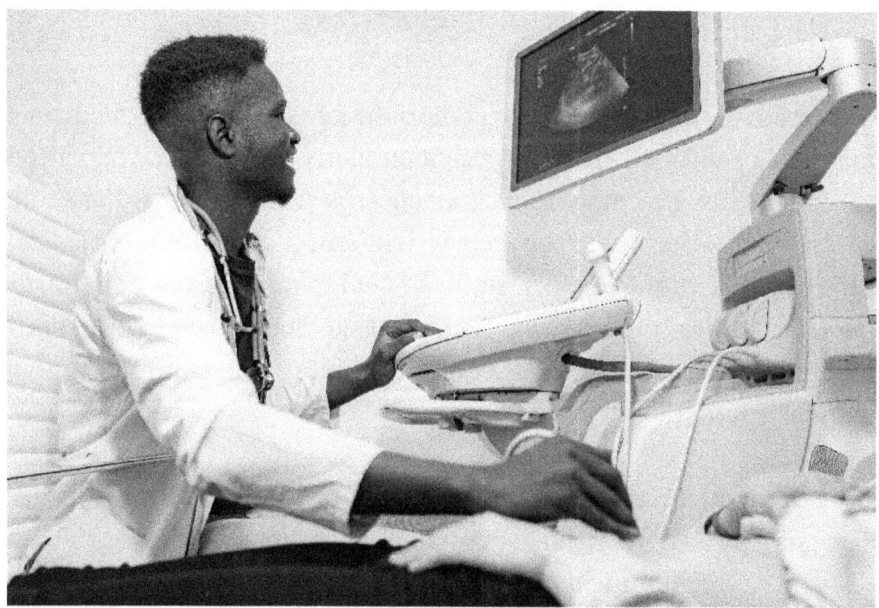

Individuals studying medicine or pursuing a medical career can attest that it is full of challenges and can be incredibly stressful. This includes very demanding coursework, years of hard studying, medical school, and residence. After all of this, the rewards can be great, such as having steady and profitable employment and touching people's lives one person at a time. This career gives a sense of fulfillment just by helping others. It includes hard hours of psychological stress. It is marked by persistent hurdles, sometimes financial issues, health problems, and other personal obstacles. The process may cause extreme adversities and stress.

People who go through demanding times likely develop exceptionally good coping skills and a deep appreciation for not only big wins but also little wins. Both routes have advantages and disadvantages of their own. The medical field is very structured and rigorous and gives few benefits, or the benefits are not usually evident. Strong network support is needed and shown, but on the other hand, it is a life of obstacles. The process may cause extreme adversities and stress. It includes many more challenges but can result in significant development and fortitude.

The road to success is also comprised of setbacks. In medicine, mistakes or difficult cases can occur similarly to failures experienced in our pursuits. Learning from experiences is crucial for growth in both cases. Both require focus and long-term objectives. Medical professionals must keep their ultimate goal in mind just as individuals pursuing success on this road. They must stay motivated despite short-term difficulties. Both fields require the ability to adapt to changing circumstances; this is vital in both cases.

In both medicine and the journey to success, unforeseen challenges can arise at any moment. Both paths teach valuable lessons about resilience, commitment, and the importance of learning from hardships.

Chapter 15

The Life of a Farmer Compared to The Road to Success is Paved With Hardships

If we compare the life of a farmer with a rocky road to success, it will include overcoming many obstacles that draw attention to different but related experiences. The farmer awaits several challenges, such as severe weather patterns or conditions, the shift of market prices, the demand for physical work, and sometimes very hard financial strains.

The task of a farmer is hard and requires rigorous living arrangements. The farmer provides a strong bond with the land, which results in self-sufficiency, and the farmer feels the fulfillment of helping to produce food. Despite their difficulties, farmers should have good work ethics and communication with their community. The path to great achievement comes with many difficulties and obstacles. Achieving success involves several financial embarrassments and some personal disappointments.

Both paths require significant effort and resilience. A farmer's life is tied to the land and cycles, whereas the road to success through hardship involves navigating personal or professional challenges. Both the farmer and the path to success offer unique challenges and rewards, shaped by the nature of the work and the obstacles encountered and overcome.

NOTES

Chapter 16

The Life of a Builder Compared With The Road to Success Paved With Hardships

Despite the differences between a builder and the road to success, both paths require a great deal of work. For the builder to make a living, it is based on him doing physical work and exercising his skills. It requires practical problem-solving and the ability to perform meticulously. The weather is sometimes one of the many difficulties that builders encounter. Sometimes the sun is raging hot, or it might be snowing or raining another time, depending on where they are. They also encounter a limited time to complete their project. They have safety concerns to make sure their job satisfaction is at its peak; they must learn to observe the real effect of their labor, making sure that your building is a long-lasting structure.

On the other hand, the path to success is not always straightforward, but it also involves many complex steps. It entails overcoming hardships and obstacles, some personal ones too. There is also a period of uncertainty. Sometimes, you don't even know if you are going or coming on this road. You have long hours and all sorts of thoughts captivating your mind. You must be able to adjust to different conditions that might make it necessary for your success.

This journey calls for persistence and resilience and living in what we call ongoing progress right here. For a builder, the journey is often immediate and rough. The road to success involves both external achievement and internal growth, which is the key to success.

Chapter 17

The Life of a Teacher Compared to the Road to Success Paved With Hardships

A common theme between the life of a teacher and the path to success is that both include major hurdles and the need for endurance. Instructors or teachers face challenges, including navigating educational policies, handling varied classroom dynamics, and attending to the needs of individual pupils.

Debrakay M. Brown

The path to achievement is often paved with obstacles and challenges that are sometimes hard to overcome. Both routes demand a dedication to long-term objectives and a drive to change the world, whether in the classroom or in pursuit of individual or professional success.

Success, such as good teaching and frequently overcoming these obstacles, requires pushing through anyway until success is achieved.

Chapter 18

The Life of a Musician Compared to the Road to Success Paved With Hardships

The life of a musician often involves a mix of creative passion and significant challenges.

Musicians typically face long hours, unpredictable income, and the pressure to constantly evolve their craft. This can include grueling practice schedules, frequent travel, and the need to handle both their careers' artistic and business sides.

On the other hand, the road to success requires first overcoming obstacles and setbacks while striving for one's goals. For musicians, this might mean dealing with rejection, financial struggles, or balancing personal and professional life, and a constant need for improvement.

Success often comes after enduring these hardships and persisting through difficulties. In essence, both parts involve a lot of hard work and resilience. A musician's journey is a vivid example of the broader concept of achieving success despite challenges. Just as a road with bumps and detours eventually leads to a destination, the musician's persistence and dedication lead to recognition and achievement.

NOTES

_____
_____
_____
_____
_____
_____
_____
_____
_____
_____
_____
_____
_____

Chapter 19

The Life of a Neonatal Intensive Care (NICU) Nurse Compared to the Road to Success Paved With Hardships

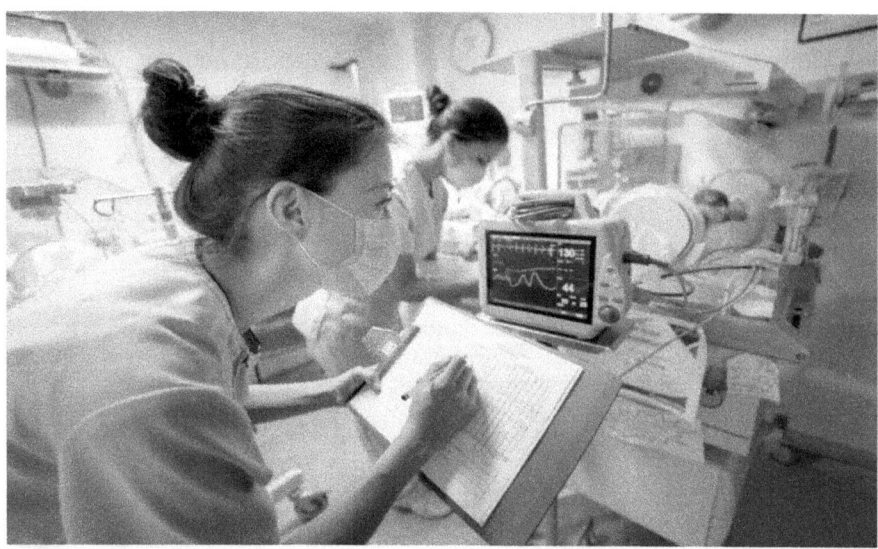

There are various ways in which being a NICU nurse is like the path to success. Both require you to navigate a difficult and tiring path. Like the NICU nurse, they must manage the emotional and physical challenges of caring for severely ill newborns while working under intense pressure.

Similarly, achieving success doesn't happen easily; instead, it is paved with disappointments and challenges that require perseverance and tenacity.

Secondly, the NICU nurse's role is marked by continuous learning and adaptation—like the journey to success—where one must constantly evolve and overcome new challenges. Both paths require devotion and the ability to handle adversity gracefully.

Finally, the NICU nurses and those striving for success on this road of hardship ultimately find that their effort is rewarded in the life-saving care of vulnerable infants, while those who persist through hardship often find their goals achieved and their efforts validated.

As Christians, our path often emphasizes perseverance through trials and the importance of hope.

NOTES

_____
_____
_____
_____
_____
_____
_____
_____
_____
_____

Chapter 20

Requirements For A Successful Journey

- We need to obey God, not our appetite (see **1 Corinthians 9:24-27**).
- We must believe God, not the deceiver (see **John 8:44**).
- We need to love God, not the world (see **1 John 2:15-17**).
- We need to worship God, not the comfort of sin (see **Habakkuk 3:17-18**).

Rules govern everything we do in life. If you are driving a car, playing a game, baking a cake, or preparing a special dish, rules govern all these, and to be successful at a game and get good results, you must stay on course and follow the rules.

As Christians, when we are born again, we are born into God's family, and it is His will that we should grow in grace and stature so we become mature in Christ. It would never be the will of God for you to remain a baby Christian from conversion, making a public declaration as you decide to be enlisted in the body of Christ. It is God's will for you to mature, read His Word, and strive to move from newborn to developing strong bones and teeth. You do not stay in one place and become a spiritual dwarf. **2 Peter 3:18** says we should grow, meaning we should grow with steady development as we increase in wisdom.

There are rules that we should observe for a good, spiritual, healthy journey on this rough, rocky road to success. An essential thing we need to do is to use the Bible—the Word of God—as our daily manual. When you purchase a new vehicle, the owner's manual comes with that vehicle. It tells you how to maintain your car. These things are non-negotiable. It instructs you about changing your oil, filling your tank with gasoline, making sure the transmission fluid is there, and your tires have adequate threads for the road. We should designate time to read the manuals to understand the car. How sad it is that we often refuse to read the Bible, our daily manual. To make this journey successful, we should apply the same principle we use to preserve the life of a car to preserve our lives and walk with Christ. The only way to preserve and enhance our Christian walk is to glorify God by spending time in His presence.

We should make it our practice to read our Bibles daily. We should not be comfortable just skimming through a few verses only when it is convenient for us. The Word of God should be on the fleshy table of our hearts while seeing to it that it remains a lamp to our feet and a light to our path. The Word corrects, comforts, and guides us on our daily path.

We should learn the true meaning of the secret of prayer, praise, and communicating with God. Every prayer we pray in sincerity will be answered. The answer might not be a "yes," and sometimes the answer is an instruction to "wait." However, there will be an answer.

We should rely on the Holy Spirit totally (see **Romans 8**). This is such comfort to the weakest of us. You should stand aside and allow the Holy Spirit to dominate all your decisions in life.

We should do our best to attend church as regularly as we can. The church is Christ's organization here on earth, and the Bible commands us to get together and worship God. Nothing can replace the requirement from God to attend church to worship God; the Word of God says, "iron sharpens iron" (see **Proverbs 27:17**). We encourage and strengthen one another when we gather in worship. If we love God, we will find it very easy to follow His commands.

Love should be the ruling principle in our lives. Jesus told us that if we follow Him, all men will know that we are His disciples if we love one another (see **John 13:35**). It is the greatest rule we should follow. As Christians, we should show love to one another. We should be obedient with no strings attached. God is with us, and we live graciously with Him.

We should always remember that we are called to be the light of this dark and sinful world. As representatives of God, the beauty of Jesus should be seen in us; His wondrous compassion and purity should be readily identifiable in us.

- We should commit ourselves and offer our flesh to death.
- We should count ourselves dead to sin but alive to God through Christ our Lord (see **Romans 6:11-12)**.
- We should live a holy life every day to succeed despite challenges. We must develop the will to survive all obstacles.

Questionnaire Mrs. P

Gender
☐ Male
☑ Female

Age
(Check the corresponding box)

☐ 20-29
☐ 30-39
☐ 40-49
☐ 50-59
☑ 60-69
☐ 70 and over

1. **Describe a challenge you faced and how you managed to overcome it.**

Answer: My son went away to college and was having difficulty adjusting. It was so bad that he was not communicating or attending classes as he should. I overcame this by getting the advisors and the housing administrators involved. Most of all, I fasted and prayed for God to help us through, and He did.

2. **Talk about a time you faced a challenging problem when you almost gave in but were rescued in the nick of time.**

Answer: My son was faced with the problem of being suspended from college because he did not do his assignments and tests and attended classes as he should. I encouraged and told him to submit a letter explaining what he was going through. He submitted that letter explaining his situation and his problems and that he could do better with a 4.0 GPA and a scholarship. We got the suspension letter on Friday, and our home was tense over the weekend. My sister in Christ and I prayed because we knew God answered. On Monday, my son got an email stating they withdrew the suspension. Who could this be but Jesus?

3. **Did this experience teach you anything? Explain.**

Answer: This experience taught me that whenever I have a problem, I need to rely on God. It reminded me that in our brokenness, through faith in God, we can be victorious. This situation allowed me to recognize an inner strength I did not even know I had.

4. **Tell of a time you had to use good judgment and quick thinking to solve a serious problem.**

Answer: I started a Science project at my school. I got the material I needed to work with long after all the other classes did. When I told my supervisor of the predicament, she turned it down and said she thought it more appropriate for another teacher to take over. It bothered me for a while because it was very clear that she wanted to highlight some weakness on my part. Sometimes, people try to set unrealistic expectations and provide little support just to see you fail.

Rather than getting discouraged, I focused on doing different projects that would show my strengths. I found an area where I was able to innovate and took the initiative to develop a project aligned with a specific goal, but at the same time, I could humbly showcase my skills. I presented my work confidently, and the feedback was overwhelmingly positive, exceeding expectations. The project became such a success that the other teachers spoke about it for weeks.

5. Did you receive the result you anticipated? Explain.

Answer: Absolutely! My belief in the importance of perseverance, even in my challenging situation, taught me that focusing on my strengths can turn adversity into opportunity.

6. Describe a time when you had to overcome an issue that only you knew about.

Answer: My father passed away suddenly in his sleep. When I received the news, I became utterly despondent because I did not get a chance to visit him that year. The emotions weighed on me so badly. I felt guilty and isolated in my grief, wanting to hide my pain from others, perhaps thinking they would not understand or would judge me. At the same time, I was still trying to deal with the loss.

7. Did this experience enhance your life's journey in any way? Explain.

Answer: This experience taught me not to put off what can be done today for another day. I would not have felt so guilty had I tried to visit my dad. We should try to stay in touch with loved ones and see them as often as possible.

8. What motivates you most in your daily walk on your personal life's journey?

Answer: I get motivated by remembering that God loves me, and I can trust Him to take me through whatever I am going through.

Trusting Him pays big dividends. My complete reliance on Him has allowed me to live a challenging but successful life.

9. Name two effective ways you have used to handle stress.

Answer: It is always great to stop and assess the situation. If one cannot change the situation, try to change your attitude. Secondly, practice mindfulness and meditation, and pray and trust God for your breakthrough.

SUMMARY OF MRS. P'S QUESTIONNAIRE

Mrs. P's son faced significant challenges in college. He was struggling emotionally with an anxiety disorder despite being a brilliant scholarship-recipient student with a 4.0 GPA. His issues with assignments and class attendance led to a suspension threat from the college. However, the suspension was unexpectedly withdrawn after she and her sister engaged in fasting and prayer. Similarly, she encountered ridicule at her workplace for a project, but she persevered and ultimately produced a top-notch outcome. She believed that while hardships manifest in various forms and people respond differently when facing challenges, faith and resilience become crucial tools in these experiences. These situations illustrate that how we confront difficulties can shape our level of success.

Let me say congratulations, Mrs. X, on your incredible journey! Your resilience in the face of adversity is truly inspiring. Despite the challenges you faced, you never gave up on your child. Through prayer and determination, you turned difficulties into stepping stones to success. Your unwavering faith and commitment have made a profound impact and are a testament to the power of perseverance.

May your story be a means of convincing someone that hardships are sometimes meant to propel you to success.

Questionnaire Lady L

Gender
☐ Male
☑ Female

Age
(Check the corresponding box)

☐ 20-29
☐ 30-39
☐ 40-49
☐ 50-59
☑ 60-69
☐ 70 and over

1. **Describe a challenge you faced and how you managed to overcome it.**

Answer: It had been a beautiful vacation, such a much-needed break as my two kids, one ten-year-old and one six-year-old, and I went abroad to a beautiful country to spend some well-needed time with my husband and their loving dad. In this quiet, beautiful country, the weather had been perfect, the air fresh, and we were all so content. Our vacation ended, and when we returned home, the reality of our lives caught up with us.

As we sought to enjoy the usual tranquility of our home in the country, the familiarity of our own home felt so good. Unfortunately, during those moments and times, things can go wrong. This particular morning, I was in my bedroom packing some clothes and other things for a needy neighbor. My younger child was outside playing with his neighborhood friends, laughing and running around, while my older son was doing his own thing in his room. I always felt a sense of comfort when they were playing together; their voices echoing in the yard always brought me joy.

Life felt peaceful, but that peacefulness would soon be shattered. As I stepped out of my room to get a bag from another part of the house, I was stopped dead in my tracks as I came face to face with a stranger. His face was hidden behind a mask; only his two eyes were visible, and in his hands, he held a gun, cold, steady, and he turned it on me.

"Don't move!" he ordered.

His voice was deep, stern, and unnerving. I was too frightened to scream. He fired two shots, which did not miss me. My heart hammered in my chest as fear washed over me like ice water. Then, in the next moment, the sound of small feet, innocent and unaware, approached from behind this stranger. My younger child, oblivious to danger, had come inside and was making his way towards us. He stopped short when he saw the man with the gun, but before he could react, the stranger took a step forward. Without warning, the gun went off. I screamed as the sound of the gunshot rang out, echoing in the narrow hallway. My mind didn't comprehend what had just happened. I didn't realize it was my son who got the shot.

As soon as the intruder fired the last shots, he started making his way outside. On his way out, my older son came out of his room when he heard the shot, but the intruder ordered him to go back to his room. The intruder ran out of sight. I ran outside and started to scream for help. It was at that time I saw my little son running behind me, screaming, *"Mommy, look! Look!"* It was then I realized that he was shot as well. At that time, I did not even remember that I was shot, but I rushed inside and grabbed towels to bind the wounds of both my child in an effort to control the heavy bleeding. My older son, whom the intruder ordered to go back to his room, escaped and bolted outside, shouting and crying for help because he saw us bleeding. I didn't even pay attention to the blood dripping from my own wounds. All I wanted to do was to get my wounded child to safety.

I grabbed my car keys, strapped my son in the car, jumped around the wheel, and started heading out to the hospital, which was two hours away. By this time, neighbors came to my rescue and took me from behind the steering, while one or two others jumped in the vehicle, and we went on our way. The pain shooting through my abdomen was terrible, but my attention was focused on my son. They could see my panic as blood kept oozing from our wounds. The man driving, knowing exactly what to do, floored the gas pedal, driving as though his life depended on it.

We arrived at the hospital as quickly as possible. The staff rushed out, and within minutes, we were receiving treatment. The doctors worked tirelessly, and I remembered the blur of their actions, the pain, and the uncertainty of whether we would survive. I didn't care about anything except my child. Hours later, I learned that my son had a long road to recovery, but he would be okay. As for me, I was stitched up and stabilized. The trauma of the event would linger, but I had survived. We had survived, and the man who had done this to us went on another rampage and was killed by police. I had no words to explain what had happened that day; I only knew that life would never be the same, and somehow, we had come through it because of love, strength, and people who cared when it mattered most.

2. **Tell of a time you had to use good judgment and quick thinking to solve a serious problem.**

Answer: I can recall when my first son was only four years old, we were all at home, but suddenly, we missed him from our company. We started running around the house searching and calling him, but he was nowhere to be found. I can remember feeling my heart beating outside of my body. I noticed a ladder leaning against the house. I calmly called him and heard him answer, *"Yes, Mommy."* The answer was coming from the top of the house. My child was on top of the house, so composed. I tried to keep him quiet while calmly coaxing him to take his time and come down. We nervously watched him as he carefully tried to put his feet on the steps of the ladder. Eventually, he made it down safely. We were all so happy and thankful that things ended without incident.

3. **Did you receive the result you anticipated? Explain.**

Answer: I certainly did. My child was safe and sound. Thanks be to God.

4. **What motivates you most in your daily walk on your personal life's journey?**

Answer: My biggest motivation on this life journey is my Christian walk with God. I remember in my earlier years, I was engulfed in poverty. The significant change in my circumstances gives me profound motivation today. The transition from extreme poverty to financial stability motivates, inspires, and gives me a sense of gratitude and purpose. It keeps my faith strong as I recognize the role of divine guidance and support from God in overcoming challenges. Being able to now give to the less fortunate while reflecting on the Christian principles of Christianity and generosity strengthens me. This motivates me daily, brings me fulfillment, and reinforces my commitment to life and to live out faith tangibly.

5. **Name two effective ways you have used to handle stress.**

Answer: Positivity and being committed to regular fasting and prayer are two effective ways. Maintaining a positive outlook can shift your focus from stressors to solutions, reducing anxiety. It helps you be resilient and begin to see challenges as opportunities for growth. Fasting and prayer help us to break from things that distract us daily. It also helps to promote self-discipline, allowing us to reflect on what is most important and reduce stress. Living prayerfully keeps us connected and offers us a true sense of peace. Together, these practices create a complete approach to managing stress.

6. **Would you say that the difficult times you experience in life have propelled you to the success you are having today? Explain why or why not.**

Answer: Absolutely. There was a time I couldn't find food to eat. I didn't have clothes. I would hide and borrow my grandmother's shoes to wear to church. I had to sneak it away, put it in a bag, and walk barefoot to the church; when I reached the church doors, I would quickly put them on and go inside. When the church was finished, I had to repeat the process of taking it off, putting it back in my bag, walking barefoot back home, and dusting the shoes off to disguise any evidence of its use. I would be in big trouble if my grandma found out I was wearing her pair of shoes that she kept safely to wear if she had to go anywhere special.

Grandma wanted me to stay home and not go to church because she could not afford to provide clothing and shoes for me to go out, but I loved church and didn't want to stay home. I can clearly remember going to school without lunch. I would walk a good distance home at lunchtime just to get one ripe banana, a piece of sugar cane, or just a dry piece of bread and water, then run back to school to ensure I reached back on time.

I lacked the basic necessities, making this a sad journey for me as a young lady growing up in the country. However, I worked hard in life and strove to be ambitious to improve my life. I was able to overcome the challenges. Challenges coupled with the hardships foster a profound appreciation for what I have now. It has built my strength and determination and allowed me to be fearless in tackling new challenges.

Understanding firsthand poverty has allowed me to develop compassion for others. All the difficulties have sharpened my focus on achieving new goals and maturing my daily achievements. When I look back on my life, I remember owning one dress, one blouse, and one skirt. Today, I have closets of clothes and shoes of all colors and fashion. From being barefoot to owning an innumerable number of shoes, it humbles and motivates me to be more and more a blessing to others.

The difficulties in my life have certainly helped to propel me to success. These challenges make me stronger and more adaptable to face other difficulties. Adversities force me to reevaluate my priorities and help me to focus on what truly matters, setting clearer, more meaningful goals.

SUMMARY FOR LADY L

This is a powerful story of resilience and faith in the face of overwhelming adversity. Mrs. A. recounts surviving a traumatic attack in her home where an intruder shot her and her six-year-old son.

Despite the harrowing ordeal, they were rushed to the hospital, where they received the medical attention they needed.

On another occasion, her older son climbed the ladder that was leaning against the house to the roof. Mrs. A. used great care and judgment to coax him down safely. Her life, before all this tragedy, was marked by severe poverty. She recalls having little to no food or clothing, often hiding or borrowing her grandmother's shoes to wear to church. Walking barefoot to church, she would secretly stash the shoes in her bag only to dust them off and return them after service. Despite these struggles, she never lost hope.

Today, she reflects on the blessings she received in owning closets full of clothes and shoes, a symbol of her hard-earned progress and her blessings from God. Her difficult past has shaped her into a compassionate person who now helps others in need. She understands the hardships of life and is motivated by the desire to make a positive impact, knowing firsthand the challenges of going without. The trials she faced have propelled her to achieve greater heights. Her story is a testament to the power of faith, perseverance, and kindness.

Congratulations and continued blessings would be my words of encouragement to you. Your story is a testament to God's faithfulness.

Questionnaire Ms. N.

Gender
- ☐ Male
- ☑ Female

Age
(Check the corresponding box)

- ☐ 20-29
- ☐ 30-39
- ☑ 40-49
- ☐ 50-59
- ☐ 60-69
- ☐ 70 and over

1. **Describe a challenge you faced and how you managed to overcome it.**

Answer: While growing up, I always felt I never belonged to my family because I was adopted. A stigma was always attached to me that I would never become 'anything good.' Consequently, in my adult years, starting in my early 20s, I went back to school on a salary, despite being very small, and attained enough qualifications to advance me through several ranks to a seat in the boardroom. I did it to overcome the negative connotations people had about me.

2. **Talk about a time you faced a challenging problem when you had almost given in but were rescued in the nick of time.**

Answer: I recall in 2016 when I separated from my child's father and had nowhere to live, my mother permitted me to live in a self-contained flat in her house. It, however, needed some renovation work. During this time, I had just completed my master's degree, and my entire savings were depleted. I lived out of the trunk of my car and would rotate my night stays at a former boss and existing colleague. One particular Friday, the workman had completed some tiling work at the apartment. The gentleman who did the renovation was to be paid. He came to my office to collect the funds because he was heading to a parish some hours away. I drove with him to the ATM, and as I walked away from the car, I found out that the balance in my account was $0.37. As I stood in the ATM, tears began streaming down my cheeks because I didn't know how to return to the car without the workman's money. Immediately, as the card was ejected from the machine, my biological brother called me and asked, "Sister, are you okay?"

I uttered the stone-cold lie, "Yes." I was never one to beg or borrow.

He went on to say, "I'm sending you some money."

I thanked him, waited a few minutes, and checked the balance in my empty account. The amount in my account was now three times the amount I needed to pay the workman. I stood there in the ATM, looking into God's embrace and divine favor. He had saved me in the nick of time.

3. **Did the experience teach you anything? Explain.**

Answer: The experience reinforced what I already knew: God is an on-time God. He made the way when my back was against the wall, and I thought it was over. I can confidently say, "With God, all things are possible."

4. **Talk of a time when you had to use good judgment and quick thinking to solve a serious problem**

Answer: I recall an occasion when the medical officers at one of the Jamaican's major public hospitals had taken industrial action, resulting in significant patient care delays. I was a junior manager then, and my director was not at work. I offered to take the lead in addressing the group of medical doctors and their representatives, knowing that things could go wrong. Before exiting my car, I prayed and asked God to fill my mouth with words that would be music to their ears.

After a brief exchange, I led the cadre of almost 75 medical doctors away from the entrance gate at the hospital to an enclosed room. I listened to their concerns and committed to bringing attention to the matter they had raised. In exchange, I asked them to return to their duties and committed to working with them and management to address their issues. This was a tremendous success.

5. **Did you receive the result you anticipated? Explain.**

Answer: Absolutely. They returned to work, and the operations at the hospital returned to normal.

6. **Describe a time when you had to overcome an issue that only you knew about.**

Answer: I struggled with serious self-doubt and battled with anxiety and internal conflict. I often wondered if I was good enough. However, if I shared this with my peers, they would laugh me to scorn. I overcame that issue and can confidently say today, *"To God be the glory, great things He has done."*

7. **Did this experience enhance your life's journey in any way? Explain.**

Answer: The self-doubt I experienced caused me to work twice as hard as I became more intentional about what I wanted to achieve. It also taught me to be self-aware and strive to be self-sufficient.

8. **What motivates you in your daily walk on your personal life journey?**

Answer: I am inspired by the young "me" who was never to excel and achieve anything good in life. My struggles of finding me and owning a space in this world have inspired me. I am inspired by the symbolism of who I am and my value system. I am inspired by the fact that I held my head high, and today I am proud. I am inspired by my son, whom I prayed for because I yearned so desperately to call someone my own; a piece of me, my belly pain. I am inspired by the successes of my core network of family members and friends to whom I look for inspiration and who I know pray diligently for me.

My biggest inspiration is my granddaughter, who one day I pray will remember me for more than a memory but someone who would have inspired and touched her life in an extraordinary, special way.

9. **Name two effective ways you have used to handle stress.**

Answer: Quiet time. Creating downtime to find my center, meditating on God's Word, and reading my favorite murder mystery books. You can read whichever material inspires you most.

10. **Would you say that the challenging times you experience in life have propelled you to the success you are today? Explain why or why not.**

Answer: Absolutely! The challenging times I have experienced (which are many) helped to shape the person I am today and will become tomorrow. I live a life of gratitude and am truly humbled by the goodness of God, who keeps running after me. I have created and am still creating a life in which I can serve others, and I strongly believe in *"service above self."* This is the measurement of my success: giving back and making a difference one person at a time.

11. **What instruction would you give someone who finds it very hard to go through rough times?**

Answer: Have faith in God. I have looked in the open skies many times during very low periods in my life and said, *"God, I know You love me and will never allow the skies to fall down on my head."* Never lose hope, and always do an act of kindness to someone regardless of the rough times you are going through. Remember, God is able. Trust His timing.

12. **Do you agree with the statement that the road to success is paved with hardships? Why or why not?**

Answer: Yes, I do. The road to success isn't only paved with hardships, but as paradoxical as it seems, it is equally paved with failures. But every setback, disappointment, and loss provides an opportunity for us to pivot and become resilient and stronger. More importantly, success is not in the absence of adversity but in our ability to overcome.

SUMMARY FOR MS. N

Miss Z. was a young lady who faced the challenge of an upbringing marked by hardship and low self-esteem. After being adopted, she resolved to improve her life by returning to school. She started living out of her car; then later, she received a small dilapidated flat from her mom that desperately needed repairs. She ambitiously juggled her job while studying. One weekend, the repairperson came to her office for payment, highlighting her financial struggles. Despite these obstacles, she persevered and earned her master's degree. Today, she holds a prestigious job and reflects on her difficult past as a source of strength that contributed to her success.

I would love to add my congratulations on your incredible achievement. Your journey from facing challenges to thriving in a high office is truly inspiring. Your determination and resilience have paid off, and this is a demonstration of your hard work and dedication. You have turned obstacles into opportunities, and your success is well deserved.

I wish you continued success as you embrace each new chapter in your life, and I hope this story will inspire someone to be courageous and strive for excellence.

Questionnaire Mrs. D

Gender
☐ Male
☑ Female

Age
(Check the corresponding box)

☐ 20-29
☐ 30-39
☐ 40-49
☑ 50-59
☐ 60-69

1. **Describe a challenge you faced and how you managed to overcome it.**

Answer: One of my most difficult challenges was standing as a mother and fighting spiritual battles for my son. I remember handling things from a natural perspective by getting angry, arguing, and using physical discipline until the Lord showed me that there was no winning that way. I overcame it after shifting to fighting in the spirit realm through prayer, fasting, and using calm communication and love.

2. **Talk about a time you faced a challenging problem when you almost gave in but were rescued in the nick of time.**

Answer: Years ago, back in Jamaica, West Indies, I made an appointment to apply for my U.S. visa. I lived in Montego Bay, which was about a three-hour drive from the capital, Kingston, where the U.S. embassy was located. I left for Kingston, having no money for the visa fees, which was a fairly large amount for me at the time. I was hoping that my mother, who lived in Kingston, would have been able to give me the money. She wasn't. I went ahead, did the interview, and got approved. The next step was to pay the fees. On my way down the set of steps outside the building—many people were going up and down—a gentleman pointed down on the ground and said, *"Is that your money?"* I picked up what was a roll of money, only to find that it was the exact amount that I needed.

3. **Did this experience teach you anything? Explain.**

Answer: Yes, it certainly did. It taught me about God's ability to provide in ways we couldn't imagine.

4. **Tell of a time you had to use good judgment and quick thinking to solve a serious problem.**

Answer: My sister and I got on a bus bound for Kingston, Jamaica. She lived in one of the most dangerous areas in the city, so being aware of your surroundings was of paramount importance. I sat in a seat immediately behind her. While we were on our way, a young man pulled out a knife and demanded my sister to give him the necklace she was wearing. She became very scared and turned around to me and asked, *"What should I do?"*

I said strongly, sternly, *"Give it to him."* I was more angry than scared. She broke it off her neck and gave it to him. He exited the bus and left her unhurt. That was indeed the best decision I ever made at that point in time.

5. **Did you receive the result you anticipated? Explain.**

Answer: Yes, my sister lost her valuable necklace, but her life was spared, and she was safe.

6. **Describe a time when you had to overcome an issue that only you knew about.**

Answer: I found that there is much wisdom in being quiet and not being too quick to speak. I lived with these feelings for a long time. I noticed positive outcomes when I waited instead of immediately expressing my feelings and thoughts.

7. **Tell of a time when you successfully used crisis management skills to come out of a major rut.**

Answer: My eldest daughter was not feeling well for a few days. One day, she began to panic, saying that she needed to go to the hospital. I quickly realized that she was about to have a panic attack and got her to calm down by talking and encouraging her. I coaxed her into taking some deep breaths. I was not about to spend my night in the ER.

8. **What motivates you most in your daily walk on your personal life's journey?**

Answer: I am super encouraged by the words that God has spoken over my life and the words He sends to me, along with confirmations from Him. That makes all the difference.

9. **Name two effective ways you have used to handle stress.**

Answer: I regularly practice looking for the good in every situation. I would look at the bigger picture and see that whatever it is, it's temporary and will pass. More often than not, many things that cause us stress are rooted in fear and pride (my humble opinion). I also take the time to find a quiet place to sit, breathe, and relax. I would analyze the situation to determine whether or not I contributed to the problem in any way and repent. If not, I will then commit it to God, knowing that I am a child of God and whatever the problem is, He can handle it.

10. **Would you say that the difficult times you experience in life have propelled you to the success you are today? Explain why or why not.**

Answer: I see where I am much stronger, wiser, more compassionate, patient, and kind to others. When you have been through it yourself, it makes you a more caring human being, and it develops your coping skills.

11. **What instructions would you give someone who finds it very hard to go through rough times?**

Answer: I highly encourage anyone going through tough times to seek a deeper relationship with God. Walking with God does not eliminate hardships but makes them easier to bear because of His promises that give us hope. I would also encourage such a person not to isolate themselves but to ask God to send trustworthy people with whom they can confide; going through things alone only amplifies the challenges.

12. **Do you agree with the statement that the road to success is paved with hardships? Why or why not?**

Answer: Yes, the road to success is paved with hardships, especially if one is marked for greatness. The greater the call, the greater the challenges.

Debrakay M. Brown

SUMMARY FOR MRS. D

Throughout Mrs. Q's life, she has faced numerous challenges and difficult circumstances that have shaped her into a wise and resilient individual. One such instance was when she witnessed her sister being robbed in a terrifying moment. Her calm advice to give the thief whatever he demanded ultimately saved her sister's life, showing her quick thinking and ability to stay composed under pressure.

As a mother, she has also been a source of strength for her children when her daughter fell seriously ill. She trusted her instincts and refrained from rushing to the ER, instead offering comforting words and medical advice that provided relief and improved her daughter's condition.

She demonstrated deep intuition and care in her relationship with her son. She learned to trust in God and take a step back in difficult situations, leading to strong communication and better results in their bond. Her faith and resilience in divine guidance have helped her navigate unforeseen challenges, allowing her to approach life exhibiting more patience and wisdom. Her journey has not been easy. She has fought countless personal and professional battles to achieve success. Each obstacle she faced only propelled her towards greater blessings, teaching her the value of perseverance, trust in God, and strength of her spirit.

Summary Of The Road To Success Is Paved With Hardships

The Road to Success emphasizes the importance of having a clear purpose in mind and action and setting specific goals. Everyone should develop a positive attitude, be determined and creative, and build strong relationships in the face of challenges and setbacks. Training should begin from birth to be successful on this journey.

Child development could be defined as a constant irreversible increase in size and development; there is also growth in psychomotor capacity. These stages are highly dependent on genetic, nutritional, and environmental factors.

Evaluation of growth and development is crucial when a physician is doing a physical examination of a patient. The early recognition or detection of growth or developmental failure helps with effective intervention in fixing the problem.

Let's look at the stages of human growth and development:

1. Fetal stage.
2. Postnatal stage.

There are five significant phases in human growth and development:

1. Infancy (neonate and up to one year of age).
2. Toddler (one to five years of age).

3. Childhood (three to eleven years). Childhood is from 3 to 8 years old, and middle childhood is from 9 to 11 years old.
4. Adolescence or teenagers (from 12 to 18 years old).
5. Adulthood.

For progress to be evident, different stages of development must be obvious. A parent becomes very worried if any sign of retardation is shown in their child. Once this is so, immediate intervention must be sought.

Parents should help their children develop positive attitudes from a tender age. That is the only way to have a dream successfully executed. It is crucial in life that you have a plan. Invest in yourself, learn from your mistakes, stay confident, and always be motivated.

You must believe in yourself and your abilities. Make a daily reminder to yourself of your goals. A good way to do this is to keep a daily journal; write your goals down on paper, state your intended goals, and then strike them off as each one is achieved. Write down your mistakes and write down the ways you can correct them and prevent yourself from making the same mistakes again.

Learn to celebrate your victories, whether they be small or large. Never let setbacks deter you from achieving what you set out to achieve. Learn to put confidence to work and strive to master the art of confidence. Remember that success is not a destination but a journey, so strive to make your journey enjoyable. To define your success, you must develop a plan and stay focused. This will help you navigate the road well. Never compare yourself to others because this journey is personal, and be reminded that the steps you take are tailored or designed just for you alone.

Never forget that there is always room for growth and improvement, and you have your specific version of success. Cultivate your own pace and rhythm in the craft of life. Create a life worth living and try to be an inspiration to someone. This makes your life more meaningful. Design your lifestyle, and never let failures hinder your progress. If you want to achieve your goals, you should be aligned with inner strength, so be mindful and smart enough to make your goals attainable and challenging.

As you journey on the rough road to success, try to maintain good stamina and stand on your footing, and with the help of God, you should be able to conquer. As you overcome the struggles, you will discover that you are creating a clearer road map to ultimate success.

Be aggressive and break down the barriers or boulders that will try to hinder you, not with your strength but with the strength of the Lord.

I can do all things through Christ which strengthens me. (Philippians 4:13 – KJV).

Don't be deceived; you cannot make this journey relying on your strength. Cast off negativity and grow your potential one step at a time; that is the secret of lasting success. Unfortunately, some people determine their success by how much money they put in the bank, the great lavish homes they build and occupy, the latest fancy cars they drive, the name-brand clothes they can purchase, and the number of degrees behind their names. Success is much more than that.

Remain true to yourself, confidently face difficult things, and never give up. Always remember the two mantras of being successful are **hard work and determination**. The pleasure of being successful is incomparable. You can have no value if you have no dream, but always remember, you can be anything you want to be.

Henry Wadsworth Longfellow, the great poet, wrote, *"The heights by great men reached and kept were not attained by sudden flight, but they while their companions slept, went toiling upward through the night."*

This is a great motivational quote for everyone to memorize and practice. Life is what you make it, sweet or bitter, hot or cold; life can be either ashes or pure gold. When your life seems like it is getting tangled, drop it in God's hands and leave it there.

Life makes a single demand on every living organism that it comes to terms with or the situation it confronts, realizing there are two ways to deal with a situation. Sometimes, you can change the situation; other times, you must change yourself.

As you journey on this road to success, however mean and difficult it seems, never try to shun it and call it hard names. It is never as bad as you think. Never listen to the faultfinders; they will find faults even in paradise. Love your journey. Whatever you put in the early stage of life is exactly what you will end up with.

Endeavor to live a life of purpose, no matter who you are. Life will never be easy, so work hard and enjoy your experience.

"Don't take life too seriously, you will never get out of it alive."
—Elbert Hubbard

Life is all of this and more **(see James 4:14):**

- **Life is a mystery.** Life is a mystery unfolding in unexpected ways and full of uncertainties. We can never predict what will happen next, and our experiences are shaped by countless variables. The unpredictability keeps us curious and questioning, leading to both challenges and growth.

- **Life is a gracious gift from God.** Life is often viewed as a gracious gift from God, a precious and unearned blessing that offers opportunities for growth, love, and purpose. The mere existence of life, with its joys and struggles, is seen as a divine creation that invites gratitude and reverence. Each moment is an opportunity to experience God's love and grace.
- **Life is a race.** Life is a race; a metaphor often used to describe the idea that life is a competitive journey where people strive to achieve success, reach goals, and overcome obstacles. Much like a race, life can be fast-paced and full of challenges requiring perseverance, hard work, and determination. However, it is also a reminder that not everyone is running the same race at the same speed. People have different paths, timelines, and definitions of success. The key is to stay focused, keep moving forward, and avoid comparing your progress to others.
- **Life is a journey.** This sentence emphasizes the idea that life is a continuous process of growth, learning, and self-discovery. The journey is not about reaching a specific endpoint but about the experiences, relationships, and lessons gained along the way. It highlights the importance of enjoying the present moment, embracing change, and navigating challenges with resilience. Each step contributes to shaping who we are and where we are headed.
- **Life is uncertain.** This statement reflects the unpredictable nature of existence. No matter how much we plan or try to control our circumstances, the future remains unknown. Events can change unexpectedly, and challenges may arise without warning. This uncertainty can be unsettling, but it also encourages adaptability, resilience, and growth. Embracing life's unpredictability allows us to stay open to our new

opportunities, appreciate the present moment, and learn to cope with the unexpected with grace.
- **Life is brief.** This statement serves as a reminder of the fleeting nature of time. It highlights that our time on earth is limited and encourages us to make the most of every moment. This awareness can inspire us to focus on what truly matters. Building meaningful relationships, pursuing passion, and living authentically. By recognizing life's brevity, we are motivated to prioritize what brings fulfillment, make positive changes, and live with purpose.
- **Death does not end it all.** This suggests that life is part of a larger ongoing journey. Even though we may face challenges, losses, or the end of certain phases, life continues in various forms through memories, legacies, and the impact we lead. This perspective can bring comfort, reminding us that change and endings are natural, but life, in some sense, is an enduring cycle. It encourages us to embrace each moment and recognize that our influence can extend beyond our own time.

Life is a story in three volumes: the **past, present,** and **future**. The **first** is finished and laid away, the **second** we are reading day by day, and the **third** and last, volume three, is locked from sight; God keeps the key.

Pray This Prayer Daily

Our God of Abraham, Isaac, and Jacob, the celestial Monarch and Creator, who is gracious, loving, and kind; my Protector, one whose faithfulness and love knows no bounds; I am incredibly grateful for your mercies, which are new to me every morning and serves as a constant reminder of your unending love for me today and every day.

Please enable me to keep moving forward with confidence, knowing that you are the one who keeps my soul safe and will always be there to support me. Lord, You are my bulwark and butler, keeping me secure whenever I enter and exit. You constantly protect me from threats and snares of the devil, both visible and invisible. You will always be the lamp unto my feet and a light unto my path as I travel down this difficult but necessary route to achievement.

Lord, I appreciate You reminding me that You are greater than my worries, uncertainties, and potential challenges on this path.

Father divine, I ask You to constantly illuminate my path with wisdom and clarity, helping me to navigate the hardships ahead with strength and resilience. Surround me with Your grace, shielding me from doubt and fear.

Lord, please grant me the courage to face the challenges, give me the insight to learn from them, and the perseverance to keep moving forward. May each obstacle be a blessing, and may each step bring me closer to my goals.

I trust Your presence to guide my actions and decisions, ensuring that I stay true to my purpose.

Thank You for Your unwavering support as I travel this road to success although hardships are inevitable, in Jesus' name. Amen.

www.ingramcontent.com/pod-product-compliance
Lightning Source LLC
Chambersburg PA
CBHW062207080426
42734CB00010B/1832